CANADIAN STUDIES TODAY

Responses from the Asia-Pacific

PANCS

PANCS MEMBERS

Pacific Asia Network of Canadian Studies (PANCS)

Indian Association for Canadian Studies
(Chair, PANCS) President: Dr. R.K. Dhawan

Association for Canadian Studies in Australia and New Zealand
President: Professor Stewart Gill

Israel Association for Canadian Studies
President: Mr. Daniel Ben-Natan

Japanese Association for Canadian Studies
President: Professor Naoharu Fujita

Korean Association for Canadian Studies
President: Professor Eugene Lee

Association for Canadian Studies in China
President: Professor Jianwen Feng

Association for Canadian Studies in Taiwan
President: Professor Cheng Feng Shih

The Fourth PANCS Seminar, Osaka

Director PANCS Seminar: Professor Yuki Shimomura
Director JACS (ICCS): Professor Yutaka Takenaka
Representative ENCS: Professor Cornelius Remie
Representative KACS: Professor Hyun Seok Yu

CANADIAN STUDIES TODAY

Responses from the Asia-Pacific

Edited by

STEWART GILL
R.K. DHAWAN

Prestige

an international publishing house

Published by
Prestige Books
Rohini, Delhi
email: prestigebooks@gmail.com

ISBN: 81-7851-066-9

PANCS gratefully acknowledges the assistance provided by DFAIT for publication of the volume

Printed at Chaman Offset Press, New Delhi 110 002

Contents

Introduction

STEWART GILL and R.K. DHAWAN

This is the second volume produced by the Pacific Asia Network in Canadian Studies. Many of the papers were given as oral presentations at the PANCS postgraduate seminar on Canada in the Asia Pacific at Emmanuel College within the University of Queensland on Canada Day, 2008 and to a large extent this volume represents the proceedings of that event. The seminar was established in order to create a forum at which postgraduate students in the Asia Pacific area could present their research. Asia has never been more important to Canada with its largest overseas diplomatic post at the High Commission in New Delhi, rising trade with the new "tiger" economies of India and China and active military involvement in Afghanistan. Consequently, the views of young Asian scholars on Canada are relevant in the further development of educational, economic and diplomatic connections in the region.

The most popular sub-discipline of Canadian Studies in the region—the study of Canadian literature is still strongly represented in this collection. This reflects the interests of the older scholars who have been the inspiration for the research through their supervision of the students and also the easier access to Canadian literature for research purposes rather than in some of the other disciplines where material is only available through travel to Canada. This volume, however, shows a shift towards some of the priorities that the Canadian Government has identified in their recently introduced "Understanding Canada" program.

Alongside papers on Canadian literary themes there are also papers on Indigenous settlements in Canada, discussing Aboriginal Title in the Canadian legal system; trade with Japan; energy and environmental issues; communication; and multiculturalism and the Canadian mosaic. These topics reflect some of the priorities in the Canadian Government programme:

- Economic Development and Competitiveness;
- Democracy, Rule of law, Human Rights;
- Managing Diversity; and,
- Environment and Energy.

The papers in the volume represent a wide variety of cultural perspectives and education systems.

Multicultural education has indeed been one of the most prominent phenomena in Canadian education, in the last two decades. It is essentially the offshoot of the concept of multiculturalism. Once we agree that Canada is a multicultural society, we assume that the key role is played by the implementation of multicultural education. It goes without saying that multicultural education can flourish only if it is accepted as the objective of social policy. The need of the hour is then to evolve and identify a conception of multicultural education which matches the goal of multiculturalism in Canada.

Canada is essentially a multicultural society. The theme of identity has been traditionally a subject of great interest. In the context of its varied problematic, the process of inventing the Canadian nation has been an ongoing process that began in the nineteenth century and these issues are alive even today. Writers like Margaret Atwood, Robert Kroetsch, Margaret Laurence (died 1987), Rudy Wiebe, and a host of other contemporary writers, through their writings—in themes, characters, narrative modes and strategies—are trying to highlight this quest for national identity by defining, redefining, analyzing and exploring it from all possible angles. The identity crisis of the protagonists in Laurence's fiction is a microcosm of the problematic of complex Canadian identity at the national level. In this connection, Laurence's views reinforce the dilemma of the complexity of this psycho-social and psycho-cultural Canadian construct:

> If our upsurge of so-called nationalism seems odd or irrelevant to outsiders, and even to some of our own people (what's all the fuss about?), they might try and understand that for many years we valued ourselves insufficiently, living as we did under the huge shadows of two dominating figures, Uncle Sam and Britannia. We have only just begun to recognize ourselves, our land, our abilities. We have only just begun to recognize our legends and to give shape to our myths.[1]

Diversity is intricately connected with the diaspora in Canada. It is an accepted and acknowledged fact of the literary history of North America in general and Canada in particular that 'Immigrant Writing' or 'Diaspora Writing' is fast emerging as a distinct and well-identifiable category. In the case of Canada, which is otherwise largely inhabited by the immigrants from all over the world, migrated population from the Asia Pacific region forms a significant segment. The situation of 'a mosaic' as against 'a melting pot' in the U.S.A. makes Canada a better sought-after destination as compared to America. Canada also occupies a unique position owing to the fact that it is one of those very few countries that have exhibited much courage in officially putting on their statute book *A Multicultural Policy and A Multicultural Act*. In fact, the policy and the Act are significant government initiatives aimed at efficient management of their ethno-cultural diversity. Used prescriptively, multiculturalism in Canada encompasses a relatively coherent set of ideas and ideals in defence of 'celebrating diversity' as a positive, central and valued component of the Canadian mosaic. The Policy and the Act have emerged due to five hundred years of continuous immigration to Canada. As a natural consequence of this, preserving of linguistic, cultural and literary heritage has endowed the Canadian society with a vibrancy and richness that several other societies lack. This is a society in which the charter groups, indigenous communities and the immigrant rub shoulders with one another in all walks of life.

A new area of research is environment and industrial growth. The interrelationship between technology and economic application is highly dynamic and interactive. The last two decades have witnessed significant changes in international societies, which in turn have made a great impact on both society and environment. While technology has transformed human life, accelerated national economy, it has caused depletion of natural resources and environmental degradation. This has posed a great challenge to the entire humanity.

It is significant to note that till the twentieth century, people were not conscious of environmental degradation. In the 1960s and 1970s, we began to learn that human activities were exceeding the world's ability to deal with the wastes they produced. Prior to that period, the atmosphere seemed too large, the oceans too deep and the forests too vast for our action to have a significant impact on them. The emergence of global environmental problems such as climate change, global warming, air pollution changed that perspective and led to the need to adopt a new approach to economic development.

One is happy to note that PANCS is probably the most diverse of any of the Canadian Studies networks operating around the globe. In many cases the presentations are by students just setting out on their postgraduate study while others are at the end of their projects and this is reflected in the papers. In every case, whether the author is commencing a thesis or has already completed, PANCS is happy to be in partnership with the young scholars in encouraging them in their research and publications. To that end, at the Osaka PANCS Seminar on 11 and 12 September, 2009 there will be a workshop conducted in order to help our graduates to develop their research, communication and publication skills.

The important unifying theme is the expansion of Canadian studies and the task of the overseas scholar bringing a reflection from the outside of what it means to be Canadian or as a famous Scottish poet put it: "To see ourselves as others see us". This is a quote from Robert Burns' poem "To a Louse, On Seeing One on a Lady's bonnet at Church":

> Oh wad some power the Giftie gie us
> To see oursels as others see us!
> It wad frae monie a blunder free us
> *An' foolish notion*

Burns had a profound understanding of human nature, in that he effectively forces us to hold up a mirror to ourselves. We need to take an honest look at ourselves and also look beyond the commonly held perceptions. The essays in this collection are offered up as part of a reflection on Canada from the Asia Pacific region.

NOTE

1. Margaret Laurence, *Heart of a Stranger* (Toronto: McClelland and Stewart, 1976), p. 217.

"So I Filled My Box of Light": Archival Risk in Early Images of Canada's Aboriginal Peoples

MIN-HSIOU RACHEL HUNG
National Sun Yat-sen University, Taiwan

The visual world of the nineteenth century that cameras produced has been considered one of immediacy and truthfulness: photographs, attached to real world referents, were linked in a chain to represent an accurate and factual world (Cronin 140). However, when we consider that the inherent accuracy was created by the mechanical workings of the photographic process, it would seem that immediacy was an illusion. Not only did the camera record what drawing could have done before, but photographs, as creations that transform distant locales and their inhabitants into fictions, conform to Western needs, beliefs and expectations (Schwartz 30). Today, nineteenth-century photographs serve as a means for contemporary viewers to connect with their ancestral and cultural pasts.

Editorial selectivity itself is significant in this process, for, as Elizabeth Edwards has argued, a photograph's "material forms," which play a crucial role in photography's relationship to memory, are "enhanced by its presentational forms" (222). In other words, the way that a compilation is put together, from the selection of images and editing techniques to the actual book in which the photographs are reproduced, help to determine how any given image will be read and understood. When considering photographs in a collection, the meaning of an image is not at all static or stable; it shifts depending on who is doing the viewing and in what context it is seen. As photography theorist Abigail

Solomon-Godeau writes, "photographic uses, and the meanings ascribed to them, are constantly in flux" (169-70). Even the most seemingly static representations are actually sites of multiple meanings: what Solomon-Godeau has termed the "surrounding editorial environment," will undoubtedly "influence the way in which these images will be read and interpreted" (179-80). Photographs taken by nineteenth-century anthropologists or human geographers of aboriginal peoples have a different set of meanings when they are stored in a national archive bureau or collected in a book as illustrations.

This essay concerns the interconnection between photography and the archive in the book *Encounters: Early Images of Canada's Aboriginal Peoples, from the Library Collections of the Geological Survey of Canada* (1996), edited by John A. Stevens. It examines an overlapping series of historical discourses, which intersect with the multiplicity of cultural transactions and photographic materialities to manufacture the after-image in the photographic archives. In Stevens' work, transcultural practices of intervention and the manipulation that occurs when documenting an "objective" reality complicate aesthetic representations of histories. At the same time, the flow of history of Canada's aboriginal peoples is interrupted and becomes messianic in the photographic presence of Stevens' work. My central concern here lies not in the problematics of referentiality, but in the controlling rule of those problematics, beginning with a focus on authenticity, collaboration, and the archival sense of ethnic agency versus political representations in the nineteenth century.

The photographic images in *Encounters* represent a small sample of the collection in the library of the Geological Survey of Canada (GSC). This sample nevertheless demonstrates the library's range of subject and detail, providing a list of materials to locate a photographic domain in which late nineteenth and early twentieth-century Canadian photographers collected almost all available aboriginal knowledge. In effect, this collection of photographic images represents an act of violence, in which the archive of the GSC was produced via a mechanism of control that charged a variety of state facilities with surveillance of aboriginal communities. In the Survey's attempt to "reveal individuals, families and nations in transition" (*Encounters* 3), the photographic images are connected to a discursive formation that, for Jacques Derrida, is archivization as a "gathering together" which "aims to coordinate a single corpus, in a system or a synchrony" and always works against itself (3).

Michel Foucault's concept of "archive" is quite distinct from the Derridean idea of an empirical data *corpus*. For Foucault, the archive is not a passive collection of records from the past. Rather, he would see the photographic images collected in *Encounters* as an active and controlling force which gives an ever-changing system "the great confused murmur" that emanates from the discursive formation (129). The massive images from the GSC had a set of meanings or a form of risk, which changed with the camera frame that photographers brought to it. The archive is not just a collection of photographs, historical documents, or transcribed descriptions, but a form of risk that "deprives us of our continuities" (131). It further establishes the fact that Aboriginal subjects and historical events are not firm and discrete entities, but dispersions across which the flows of power transverse. Relying on a set of rules that, at a given period and for a given society, defined limits and forms, the risk expresses, conserves, memorizes, and reactivates the archive (Foucault, "Politics and the Study of Discourse").

I read the photographs and descriptions in *Encounters*, examining its use of early photographic collections from western Canada and the Arctic. I argue that these photographic images are not concerned simply with accumulating, sorting, interpreting, or describing aboriginal peoples, though they may engage in these practices. They also open up temporal experiences of the virtual, described by Foucault as a "tracing-back to the original precursors, towards the search for a new type of rationality and its various effects" (4). Using Jacques Derrida's estimation on the future of the archive, and Eduardo Cadava's meditations on Benjamin's discussions of the flashes and images of history, this essay enacts a mode of archival play on history—neither linear nor successive, but rather discontinuous—constructed from what Benjamin calls "dialectical images." While the photographs of aboriginal peoples may help to constitute the reality of historical ethnic experiences, the future of the archive cannot be confined to the domain of the actual. The photographic archive as an interlocutor of violence, which emerges from the surface narrative, allows the promise of the virtual to break through, subverting the histories of the recorded being and at the same time allowing an ethnic gaze into the archive's inter-discoursivity. My argument here is that the archive functions by making risks in the particular categories by which the document has been organized, to create a different category for those photographs. The archival risk renders photographs un-developed, returning to the virtual state, to re-image them in another manner. If history as revealed by the GSC is the collective document made by a particular group of scientists and technicians, then archival work is a risk composed of the same photographs collected and arranged in a different manner.

In its investigation of the informative impact on a viewer and the mnemonic effect of the photograph, the critical literature on photography has been characterized by a tension between memory and counter-memory themes; we see this in examples of Roland Barthes and Susan Sontag. This tension is ongoing, for example, in arguments to see the photograph as the perfect tool to relieve the burden of memory on the one hand, and yet be appropriate for Sontag's photographic mnemonics on the other.

It is, however, no more acute than in the reception of the photographic archive by Allen Sekula, who foreshadows the archival struggle to accommodate order on the chaos of collectible detail in reference to photographic multilayered artifacts. In his seminal essay, "The Body and the Archive" (1986), Sekula claims that photography modifies the referent and so changes perception of its material existence: "Photography promises an enhanced mastery of nature, but photography also threatens conflagration and anarchy, an incendiary leveling of the existing cultural order" (4). The concept resembles the argument by Richard Crownshaw in "Reconsidering Postmemory: Photography, the Archive, and Post-Holocaust Memory in W. G. Sebald's Austerlitz," that archival ruination blasts the historical continuum. Calling up a Derridean reading of Barthesian counter-memory Crownshaw writes, "Working against itself, the archive works towards the eradication of memory, towards forgetting" (219). The archive works against itself from the beginning, destroys itself from the beginning, and even erases itself without trace.

For Sekula, an archival project of photography is an act of transforming photographic images to exceed the limited and fixed inscriptions with which they have been made. In effect, "the archive attempts to exist as a potent single image, and the single image attempts to achieve the authority of the archive, of the general, abstract proposition"; "the collapsed version of the archive" is threatened with falling into oblivion (Sekula 54). The inherently obsolete nature of archivization can be explained simply, as with the terminology of "a single corpus" so strikingly evident in Jacques Derrida's description of the archive's dynamic—memory and counter-memory in Archive Fever. This is ultimately an act of violence, which disrupts from within the coherence of the referent and its photographic archive. As Sekula would argue, "every proper portrait has its lurking, objectifying inverse in the files of the police" (7), and as Petra Dreiser notes insightfully, the all-encompassing corpus of images in the archive makes "no mass of information" possible "without its little holes and pricks, its suggestive absences and lurking presences" (189). Dreiser's use of a Barthesian paradigm of wounding to read the photographic archive helps us arrive at an understanding of Derrida's "archive fever," in which there is no preservation without ruination, "which permits and conditions archivization" (11-12). "The death drive is not a principle. It even threatens every principality, every archontic primacy, every archival desire. It is what we will call, later on, le mal d'archive, 'archive fever'" (12).

Whereas Stevens attempts to find the reality of aboriginal peoples of the nineteenth century across the photographic archive at the GSC, Derrida would consider Stevens' archivization as consignation which "aims to coordinate a single corpus, in a system in which all the elements articulate the unity of an ideal configuration" which has no heterogeneity (3). For Derrida, "a priori, forgetfulness and the archiviolithic into the heart of the monument" (12), is introduced to archive further when the monumentalism remembers and forgets. So, Stevens' photographic archivization is not only "anarchic, anarchontic" but also "anarchivic" or "archiviolithic" (10). Due to the unwieldy nature of the archive, totalization is desirable insofar as the archive strives for finiteness and inclusive completeness. However, the concept of the archive "violates and does violence to itself but it also institutes itself as violence. It becomes what it is, the very violence—that it does to itself" (Derrida 78). A photographic archive such as *Encounters* is only the very beginning of history work, which already lays claim to its status as the future of the past, conceptually. Indeed, it is Stevens' archival play that offers insight into Canadian multi-cultural studies and aesthetics. Albeit suggestively, he wants to allow already captured subjects the possibility of maintaining their ambiguities, to be the historical images they have been made to specify. However, Derrida might think of Stevens' working process as one that struggles to break the camera's literal hold on the subjects. More precisely, we might say his archival materials, as much of Stevens' work with the archival dynamic of the photographs involves not only preserving ethnic others, but working against itself.

Such a working-against-itself may, of course, only engender more archives: as Derrida puts it, "The archivist produces more archive . . . that is why the archive is never closed. It opens out of the future" (68). Though supposedly a repository of the past, "the future of the archive" (Crownshaw 234), violates itself from the very beginning: "it violates and does violence to itself but it also institutes itself as violence. It becomes what it is, the very violence—that it does to itself" (Derrida 78). Violence characterizes the future of the archive for Derrida; we are meant to understand, as Crownshaw would have it, "the thorough convolution of time, its dislocation, captured in the photograph, promises not only deliverance from historicism but also the possibilities of future memory work not consumed by a perfectly conceived, monumental, and therefore violent, archive" (233). The violence to the archive can thus be understood as an immanent force of resistance to the unified finite. What is important in all the theoretical attempts to explicate the potential dynamics of the futural archive, and to grasp at the deluging but fleeting instances of monumentalism, is to think of Walter Benjamin's messianic in a material way. To explore such acts of revolutionary retelling, Crownshaw brings together Benjamin and Derrida. Both see the messianic of the archive and history as means of "thinking the convolution of time" "in the belated return of the past, found in the photograph, and in the consequent generation of its shocking affectiveness" (Crownshaw 233).

On the back cover of *Encounters*, the sentences of an unknown photographer address an immediacy found in the nineteenth-century camera work: "I travelled far and the land stood up and spoke to me: I am forgetting who I am, but I still remember knowing. So I filled my box of light and carried her faces home. They speak again and now I hear and know a little of who we are." This immediacy blends a historical tracing-back process with the mnemonic effect of photography.

As editor of the collection, Stevens finds that "the Survey has amassed a priceless collection of over half a million images preserving a record of the land" (3). Geologists of survey parties, as well as photographers "taking cameras, with their fragile glass plates, into the wilderness," then speak of "the life and natural processes" (3) to reclaim images of individuals, families and tribal communities from stereotyping by the dominant culture. Stevens notes that the explanatory text that accompanies each photograph, which has been added as an intervening agent, is presented exactly as "originally written by Geological Survey officers" (3). In his brief introduction, written for twenty-first century readers, Stevens apologizes for this text, which reveals the assumptions held by nineteenth-century geologists about native people that no longer remain acceptable today. However, Stevens still claims that the connection between words and images is made in "the interests of historical accuracy" (3). The holdings at the GSC, which support research, educational, artistic and commercial purposes, are predicated on the need to project historical evidence. This mandate of the GSC leads the viewer to rely on the desire for agency and accuracy in the collection which, Stevens remarks, has to be "unaltered" and dominates its representation of nineteenth-century history: "These photographs constitute an *irreplaceable* record of an encounter between peoples, and the best of them recognize and salute the heart and soul of the stranger" (3; emphasis mine).

Photographers have played a role in the long history of Aboriginal peoples in North America. While archives held documentary images of indigeneity, however, no irreplaceable database seemed to possess the complete work of the photographers. The photos of the Earth Sciences Sector (ESS) of the GSC focus public attention on Canada's aboriginal peoples, so Stevens' research into how geographers worked and their scientific achievements has been seen as a corrective to the neglect of an earlier generation of ethnographic anthropologists. Changing attitudes to ethnic photographs as a set of historical practices, however, tends to become a political and aesthetic issue, and photographic records can add to the perplexities of cultural disconnections when they are viewed at the present juncture of ideas. These photographs not only reflect Stevens' preference for re-collecting the past, but also convey recurring structured forms and expositions in time.

By placing early images of nineteenth-century aboriginal

peoples in dialogue with the concealed implications of the GSC's archival work, I suggest that a certain strain of the virtual image enacts an after-image, an image to come, or an imaging—a haunting of the materialist image—with a dialectical and associative relationship to the messianic. At the same time, it also uncovers the trace of the other within documents that have come down to us through practices of archiving, of making images visible for the viewers. In Walter Benjamin's terms, in a viewer's origin-tracing desire for "the tiny spark of contingency" ("Small" 243) or for "something new and strange" ("Small" 242) in the photograph, "in the immediacy of that long-forgotten moment the future subsists so eloquently that we, looking back, may rediscover it" ("Small" 243). Images of the past are solicitous and desirous spectres that have not finished those past moments, which need the act of seeing in their unfinished after-images.

In Stevens' compilation and interpretation, photographs and their accompanying texts are unceremoniously buried or even unburied; however, the history returns to be seen because it is Stevens who wants something of them. It is not so much the photographs of the aboriginal peoples that tell history. If we think of the viewers who obsessively retrieve photographs from *Encounters* to look for history in the after-images, this archive of the past is a ghostly haunting of history. Stevens' work demands that we interrogate an alternative history, one that seems to have been there and then, but may not be traced back by a compilation of photographs. In other words, an after-image of the photograph is a dialectical image, by which we imagine bridges across our differences to the framed image, but also recognize what is abandoned, left behind and beyond.

Stevens' use of the word "irreplaceable" might seem reasonable in the context of a collection of photographs and words governing the seen and the stated in the past. And indeed, as if acknowledging this, he admits that "the names of many of the people in these photographs have been lost," and the GSC encourages the viewers to help identify them (3). While Stevens prefers to identify the subjects, in each photograph there exists a uniqueness that notes photography's documentary relation to an archive record, one that sets a supposedly factual moment in the nineteenth century. In Foucault's discussion of the archive and photography, photographs have long served to reveal "the appearance of a statement as a unique event" (129). *Encounters* aims to offer us photographs by which what is "seen" by cameras and what is stated by observers govern the existence of the subjects, to dictate a direct and unique reference to substantiated existences or assumed realities in the nineteenth century. However, claiming that the book is an irreplaceable reference raises a key question: what counts as a unique event for a photographic image? This collection, a printed inscription, was published in conjunction with the ESS Photo Database, a mechanical medium, which contains more than 7,000 digital images selected from the GSC photo collection. Most photographs in the book, which effectively demonstrate the unifying power of photography, can also be seen as Stevens' indomitable will and spirited sense of mission to record a unique vision of another era from another region.

However, as the ESS Photo Database instructs its public users, the search system itself (at http://geoscan.ess.nrcan.gc.ca/starweb/essphoto/servlet.starweb?path=essphoto/essphoto_e.web) classifies over 520,000 images of geo-science, geography, flora, fauna and ethno-geography dating from the 1860s, into six input boxes. To access the database, a viewer must enter one or more search terms in Keywords, Caption, Photographer, Photo Number, Publication Date, or Exclude input boxes. The process of finding a particular photograph is only possible when the viewer can deploy discrete, quantifiable, and verified knowledge to conform to the governing principles of massive data set. In *The Imperial Archive*, which discusses the origins of the archival impulse in nineteenth-century Victorian England, the prime time of British imperialism, Thomas Richards remarks that the objectives of unification in such rules for distributing accumulated knowledge are attended by ideological manipulation: "Unawares, the archival gaze has combined the triple register of inquiry, measure and examination to prepare data to be acted upon by the variable modalities of power" (Richards 116). The database search system of the GSC raises the possibility that the series of photographs is an event which does not compose to discover the past, but instead exposes the principles by which the photographs could be retrieved. Foucault explains the positivity of such governing principles: "The document . . . is no longer for history an inert material through which it tries to reconstitute what men have done or said, the events of which only the trace remains; history is now trying to define within the documentary material itself unities, totalities, series, relations" (7).

The relationship of the photographs in the ESS Photo Database to this positivity further raises the question of how to translate the seen and the stated, while the Database simultaneously documents evidence and makes workable the system of organizing the documents. The archival work in the GSC is about transformation, and is ultimately the work of translation. To some degree, the archivist is like a translator. Much of Stevens' work involves preserving the foreignness and ambiguities of found photographs, yet, his work revises what is seen and understood. In Walter Benjamin's articulation of the relation between the original and the translatable, translatability is "a renewal of something living" in which "the original undergoes a change" ("Task" 73). The images of aboriginal peoples governed by the GSC are to a large extent translated by and translatable for the search system by which photographs have been collected, stored, used and displaced. With the passage of time, the original motive for a photograph may disappear, leaving it accessible to translation in new contexts.

In the case of *Encounters*, the use of caption and photo number is important. Most of the photographs collected in the book were taken during the travels and expeditions of anthropologists and geologists to northern Canada; the tradition of using the camera to demonstrate difference and negotiate cultural relations has a long history that must be considered here. From the early days of photography, European travellers and anthropologists to the Americas began to take pictures of the aboriginal peoples on the land. The photographs in the GSC are significant because of the archive's collectivity and veracity; historiographic pictures of the strange lands could now be accessible for viewers like me in Taiwan.

With its invention, the camera and its views of distant people and places, conveyed a "new authenticity" that previous visual traditions could not offer (Wells 60). However, in the archive, this authenticity has resulted from precisely those photographic panels and tableaux that have opened archival documents up to risk. As a recording device, the ESS Photo Database Search System produces photographs and therefore makes available *a priori* copies of the moment of creation. With the capacity for reproducing what was seen, photographs found using the Search System become material and therefore archival for institutional, industrial, and cultural purposes, although it is important not to see the photographic images as the products of a continuous and diligent political strategy. Indeed, while the photographs retrieved from the GSC depict the buried past, "the law of what can be said" paradoxically communicates a virtual image, "a specific history that does not refer it back to the laws of an alien development" (127).

The GSC's educational undertakings are significant in that they mediate photography's ability to conjure a lifelike presence from the past. From A. P. Low's *Report on the Dominion Government Expedition to Hudson Bay and the Arctic Islands on Board the D.G.S. Neptune, 1903-1904*, Stevens juxtaposes a textual passage about an encounter between tribes on the island of Sagdlingmuit, close to Hudson Bay, with a photograph that has the caption, "The murderer's wife" (*Encounters* 12). The concern here, of recovering a history of 68 people in Sagdlingmuit who died of starvation and disease during the winter of 1902, lends a victim's innocence to the murderer's wife in the photograph. However, the history referred back by the five keywords—aboriginal people, Inuit, woman, female, and family—does not include the photograph of "Tattooed Aivillik woman" (Igluirmuit, Southampton Island, Hudson's Bay, A.P. Low, 1903-4) (*Encounters* 23).

To recognize the *a priori* that is accessible in the archive, the viewer must depart from it with an understanding that what is accessible is not only the image-then itself, but an image that is still to come. Consider another example of what occurs in the archiving process. Within the atemporal structure of the archive survives an untitled photograph from A.P. Low's expedition in 1903-4. Stevens could have quoted a passage from Reginald Auger's *Labrador Inuit and Europeans in the Strait of Belle Isle: from the Written Sources to the Archaeological Evidence* (1991) to make actual his "ambition to achieve a better understanding of the acculturation experienced by the Inuit during early contact with Europeans" (*Encounters* 20). The relevance of this photograph to the text does not justify allowing it more than 80 years of belated exposure time; but this, "a form of dispersion in time" (127), does emphasize the inherent selectivity of archival work.

The archival work, as such, is inaccessible to the senses. This does not, however, preclude figuring it, or constructing images from it. To the contrary, to make visible the lost past requires an archivization of images. The archive that cannot be catalogorized also cannot but be catalogized. When exhibitions of its effects are multi-catalogized, the archive appears at risk. Its risk is in the flips between the photographs, and on the surfaces among them. The photographs make the archive appear, not in their content or form (that is, not in the connotation behind the photograph or how the photographs deliver a unifying denotation), but in risk, in their classifying or cataloguing.

The archive appears in the transformations and layers of classified files, in the movement from one file to another. The risk is in the classifying and de-classifying of photographs. This is the case whether the photograph has a text caption, as in an example of a killer's wife, or not. No one kind of photograph, let alone any photograph itself, can render the archive. Since the archive exists in its classifications and declassifications, the only way a photograph can approach the archive is to multiply itself internally by a group of rules: "these rules are not imposed from the outside on the elements that they relate together; they are caught up in the very things that they connect" (Foucault 127). The rules apply in each finding from the GSC. At a certain point, the rules all cluster together. Photographers' names, photograph numbers, captions, and so on all fall apart from themselves into self-referential encompassment. The past projects ahead to multiple futures and then goes back into the moment. The archival work now engenders the virtual.

Both Benjamin and Derrida move back and forth between messianic power and disruption in seeing history to find an appropriate paradigm for re-reading the past and effecting change in the present. Derrida sees the messianic as enhancing the future of the archive: "A spectral messianicity is at work in the concept of the archive" (36). For Derrida, seeing the future "without seeing anything come" does not make the future archive a continuum of the past and present archive; rather "the doors to the future remain properly disorientating" (69). Benjamin's concept of the messianic promises the redemption of history and helps to achieve an immanent disorientation in the future archive. As Benjamin contemplates in "Theses on the Philosophy of History," "our coming was expected on earth. Like every generation that preceded us, we have been endowed with a *weak* Messianic power, a power to which the past has a claim. This claim cannot be settled cheaply" ("Theses" 254; emph. Benjamin's). The messianic in the present becomes a power that emits certain moments abbreviated from history, a power that enacts Barthes's *punctum* and Derrida's archival violence to "blast open the continuum of history" ("Theses" 262). For Benjamin, when a historical materialist redeems history, writing critical commentaries about the past to interrupt the present and disrupt historical progress, the task itself is messianic. Benjamin offers a provisional explanation for understanding what history must be conceived: "history is the subject of a structure whose site is not homogeneous, empty time, but time filled by the presence of the now" ("Theses" 261).

By placing Benjamin's "Messianic power" of history in dialogue with Jean-Luc Nancy's interrogation of the concealed mnemonic implications of the historian's work, Eduardo Cadava suggests that a certain strain of writing history circumstantiates a historical context that "history itself may never completely comprehend" (63). As a moment in the past works to uncover the trace of the other, in this case within the archive that come to us through photography, "to articulate the past historically does not mean to recognize it 'the way it really was'. . . . It means to seize hold of a memory as it flashes up at a moment of danger" ("Theses" 255). Jean-Luc Nancy then explains how the photographer as historian grasps the moment in reference to the seen and the said: "The historian's work—which is never a work of memory—is a work of representation in many senses, but it is representation with respect to something that is not representable, and that is history itself. History is unrepresentable, not in the sense that it would be some presence hidden behind the representation, but because it is the *coming* into presence, as event" (166).

As the messianic, history enacting "the coming into presence," or "the event of the promise" (Cadava 66) can be seized only "as an image which flashes up at the instant when it can be recognized and is never seen again" ("Theses" 255). As Andrew Benjamin acknowledges, the messianic, much like the phantasmal reincarnation of a past event, a moment of metempsychosis that we experience in the present, becomes a figure for the "afterlife" of a repressed or forgotten event (41). In seeking to recover those elements of the past that have been excluded as fugitive and discontinuous, writing critical histories that rescue representative potentials from the past, means writing those that multiply details rather than homogenize them. Recognizing "a past charged with the time of the now" as it blasts out of "the continuum of history" ("Theses" 261), becomes a mode of historiography, an act of archival violence that disrupts history, which invokes reified and ascribed social discourse.

Returning to the archival risk of the GSC's work, as the after-image of the lived aboriginal peoples in Canada or as instances in which the photographs become haunted by apparitions, we may speculate on the concept of virtual image in a material way. Stevens' work helps us to find instances of elision and fragmentation that exist in *Encounters*. In such moments, we do not simply study history; we experience a kind of future-history. The dialectical image as an apparition of some past moment, flickering like "a box of light," persists in the viewer's visual impressions after the scene of the past cannot be seen any longer. Such a delusive reading of the dialectical image of photographs as I have presented in this essay argues that Stevens' work, albeit unconsciously, leaves an after-image on contemporary Canadian memory of ethnicity. This memory remains in the process of colonial projects, and is politically expedient in view of the subtle colonizing tactics hidden under the umbrella of multicultural politics and practised by historical or archivist recoveries. The contribution of the ESS Database lies in the context of cultural mnemonics, in which the historiography of the killer's wife's portrait acts as a repository of the layered effects of time, accumulating a record of traces in the cultural memory of the emergent Hudson Bay of the nineteenth century. The cultural mnemonics of the historiography represented by Stevens is a conflation of historical memory in the archive, and working through the archive. The apocalyptic and promising future of the archive, nevertheless, is not fulfilled by the narrated ethnic gaze, but in a space that-has-not-been in which the viewer's gaze is found by gazing back at a moment past, in a coming present marked only as after-image.

Works Cited

Benjamin, Andrew. *Present Hope: Philosophy, Architecture, Judaism*. New York: Routledge, 1997.

Benjamin, Walter. "A Small History of Photography." *One-Way Street, Other Writings*. Trans. Edmund Jephcott and Kingsley Shorter. London: Verso, 1979.

_____. "The Task of the Translator." *Illuminations*. Ed. Hannah Arendt. New York: Schoken, 1989. 69-82.

_____. "Theses on the Philosophy of History." *Illustrations*. Ed. Hannah Arendt. Trans. Harry Zohn. New York: Schocken, 1968. 253-64.

Cadava, Eduardo. *Works of Light: Theses on the Photography of History*. Princeton: Princeton UP, 1997.

Crownshaw, Richard. "Reconsidering Postmemory: Photography, the Archive, and Post-Holocaust Memory in W.G. Sebald's Austerlitz." *Mosaic* 37.4 (December 2004): 215-36.

Derrida, Jacques. *Archive Fever: A Freudian Impression*. Trans. Eric Prenowitz. Chicago: U of Chicago P, 1996.

Dreiser, Petra. "Black, Not Blank: Photography's (Invisible) Archives in John Edgar Wideman's Two Cities." *Mosaic* 37.4 (December 2004): 185-201.

Edwards, Elizabeth. "Photographs as Objects of Memory." *Material Memories: Design and Evocation*. Ed. Marius Kwint, Christopher Breward, and Jeremy Aynsley. Oxford: Berg, 1999.

Foucault, Michel. *The Archaeology of Knowledge and the Discourse on Language*. Trans. A.M. Sheridan Smith. New York: Pantheon, 1972.

Nancy, Jean-Luc. "Finite History." *The States of Theory*. Ed. David Carroll. New York: Columbia UP, 1990. 149-72.

Richards, Thomas. *The Imperial Archive: Knowledge and the Fantasy of Empire*. London: Verso, 1993.

Schwartz, Joan. "The Geography Lesson: Photographs and the Construction of Imaginative Geographies." *Journal of Historical Geography* 22.1 (1996): 15-45.

Sekula, Allan. "The Body and the Archive." *October* 39 (1986): 3-64.

Solomon-Godeau, Abigail. "Who is Speaking Thus? Some Questions about Documentary Photography." *Photography at the Dock: Es-*

says on Photographic History, Institutions, and Practices. Minneapolis: U of Minneapolis P, 1991. 169-83.

Well, Liz, ed. *Photography: A Critical Introduction.* 2nd ed. London: Routledge, 1998.

Indigenous Settlements in Canada: Aboriginal Title in the Canadian Legal System

AWI MONA, CHIH-WEI TSAI
National Taitung University
Graduate Institute of Austronesian Studies

> All landscapes have a history, much the same as people exist within cultures, even tribes. There are distinct voices, languages that belong to particular areas. There are voices inside rocks, shallow washes, shifting skies; they are not silent. And there is movement, not always the violent motion of earthquakes associated with the earth's motion or the steady unseen swirl through the heavens, but other motion, subtle, unseen, like breathing.
>
> Joy Harjo, *Secrets from the Centre of the World*[1]

Introduction

In considering the relationship between the private property rights and the State's sovereignty, it is useful to trace back to two different historical backgrounds on this vast continent of North America. On one hand, before the Canadian State acquired this continent, it is observed by the Canadian precursors, the English colonizers, that all lands were held by some lord, and ultimately by the Crown. It could be understood as the legacy of English feudalism.[2] In the Canada, the legal theory of landownership has been that the sovereign owns all land for the benefit of the people of the realm and that the sovereign grants out rights in that land to subjects, who hold that land under the sovereign's paramount superiority.[3] Upon the completion of the Canadian Constitution, the Parliament enjoys the sole power for the dispositions and regulations of all territories and properties belonging to the Canada.[4] Consequently, individual rights in land are derived from the government.

On the other hand, this immense turtle land was owned by the aboriginal nations from the time immemorial.[5] For most Canadians, it is a misconception that they acquired this continent by discovery or the concept of first possession. Most of lands in the Canada were alienated from tribal ownership to the Union of Canada through treaties and purchase. Therefore, the origin of property rights has to trace back to the interactions and relationships between various aboriginal nations and the Canadian government.[6]

Dating from the late fifteenth century onward, indigenous peoples in the New World subjected to European colonization have strived to focus national and international attention on their subjugation and dispossession. There various movements, primarily in Australia, Canada, New Zealand, South America, and the United States, began in different places at different times over the past several decades. Since the 1823 American judicial decision recognizing common law aboriginal title to the 2001 international judgment affirming aboriginal right to lands and resources, the debate of aboriginal land rights have evolved and lingered across the globe over the past two centuries.

The issue of indigenous peoples' rights, particularly in relation to land rights, sovereignty and justice has become increasingly important on the political agenda and legal landscape in Canada. This paper is devoted to identify what roles the legal and political institutions and processes imposed upon aboriginal peoples play in a continuing process of colonial domination, as well as to the construction of the distinct link that Canadian aboriginal nations have with land.

I. Aboriginal Title in the Historical Web

Aboriginal struggle for land rights mostly has been defined by the common law doctrines of "discovery and conquest" and the doctrine of "*terra nullius*."[7] With respect to the aboriginal title law, a better approach starts with the work by a famous theorist, Francisco de Vitoria. In his academic work, *De Indis et de Iure Belli Relections*, he advocated that because the Pope "has no power to temporal power over the Indian aborigines or over other unbelievers," a legitimate title to their lands could not be acquired "through the Supreme Pontiff."[8] Vitoria developed his arguments by asking the questions of "whether the aborigines in question were true owners in both private and public law before the arrival of the Spaniards."[9] He asserted that "the aborigines undoubtedly had true dominion in both public and private matters, just like Christians, and that neither their princes nor private persons could be despoiled of their property on the ground of their not being true owners" and that "certain basic rights inhere in men *as men*, not by reason of their race, creed, or colour, but by reason of their humanity."[10] Central to Vitoria's philosophy, Vitoria asserted that Indians of America possessed natural legal rights as free as rational people and had inherent rights under natural law to the territory they occupied.[11]

Vitoria's philosophy of Indian rights to land established the foundation for subsequent development in the contemporary Anglo-Commonwealth.[12] Of general importance are works written by leading Native American legal scholars, such as Vine Deloria Jr.,[13] and Robert A. Williams Jr.[14] in the United States as well as James (Sákéj) Youngblood Henderson[15] and John Borrows in Canada.

II. Aboriginal Title in the Canadian Legal Framework

As Professor McNeil pointed out, "most of the territories that eventually came to make up the British Empire were already inhabited at the time they were colonized."[16] When the Portuguese and Spanish made voyages to the New World in the fifteenth century, aboriginal peoples were already there, using lands in accordance with their own needs and their own ways of life, as people everywhere do. What impact, then, did these colonial powers have brought upon aboriginal title to land?

Aboriginal title shapes one of the most intriguing and rapidly developing areas of national law in most pre-colonized States. Over the past five decades or so, the highest court in Canada is debating with issues of proof, recognition and extinguishment of aboriginal title. Initially, aboriginal and European governments and legal systems were autonomous and independent of each other. However, as a result of a number of factors (including such factors as disease and European political attitudes towards non-Christian peoples), England and subsequent Canadian colonial governments began to successfully assert legal jurisdiction over the governments and legal systems of the aboriginal peoples.[17]

1. 1763 Royal Proclamation and the Aboriginal Peoples

Following the conclusion of the Treaty of Paris in 1763, the British Crown asserted the Royal Proclamation of 1763 aiming to exert its control over the North American colonies. The 1763 Proclamation consisted of five major parts, including provisions dealt with "purpose," "new governments to have general assemblies and make laws," "grants for settlement," "soldier settlement," and "the Indian provisions."[18] The Royal Proclamation is a Prerogative instrument. It is argued that the Royal Proclamation enjoyed the force and effect of an Imperial statute in the colonies to which it applied.[19] The Royal Proclamation had two main goals, namely:

a. To provide for the establishment of government in the territories acquired by Britain;
b. To provide for British control of Indian affairs in the new lands.[20]

With regards to its Indian provisions, the Royal Proclamation reads:

> And whereas it is just and reasonable, and essential to our interest and the security of our colonies, that the several nations or tribes of

> Indians with whom we are connected, and who live under our protection should not be molested or disturbed in the possession of such parts of our dominions and territories as, not having been ceded to or purchased by us, are reserved to them, or any of them, as their hunting-grounds; we do therefore, with the advice of our Privy Council, declare it to be our royal will and pleasure, that no Governor or commander in Chief, in any of our colonies . . . or plantations in America do presume for the present, and until our further pleasure to be known, to grant warrants of survey or pass patents for any lands beyond the heads or sources of any of the rivers which fall into the Atlantic Ocean from the west or northwest; or upon any lands whatever, which, not having been ceded to or purchased by us, as aforesaid, are reserved to the said Indians.[21]

By the 1763 Proclamation, the King "reserved" the lands west of the Appalachian height of land for the Indians. White settlers were forbidden to enter into land negotiations with the Indians, and settlement was forbidden. In Canada, the Proclamation is a key historical document and is considered the basis of the legal nature of Indian title and an historical root of the treaty process.[22]

Indian treaties are a special kind of document. In their early understandings, the British at least prior to the 1800s, regarded aboriginal nations as independent and autonomous and that treaties were in the nature of compacts between nation-states.[23] As noted by Professor Borrows that the Proclamation characterized the relationship between the Crown and aboriginal peoples as one between sovereign entities coexisting in a peaceful, reciprocal, and mutually beneficial manner. The Proclamation's description of "the several Nations or Tribes with whom we are connected, and who live under our Protection" indicated that the Aboriginal peoples were not subjects of the Crown, but allied nations.[24]

Conversely, one of the most critical misunderstandings of treaty process was interpretation. Given the great gulf between aboriginal and English concepts and language, any English written treaty which presumes that aboriginal nations voluntarily submitted to the English sovereign must be viewed with great scepticism.[25] If treaties are solemn compacts between independent nations, and that the rights and obligations of each nation are dependent on the agreement, how is it then that the English Crown can unilaterally assert sovereignty over a given territory which has been the subject of a treaty? A general judicial understanding of Canada showed that despite the fact that treaties were originally entered into as nation to nation compacts, i.e. international agreements, the domestic Canadian courts have not recognized them as such.[26] According to Canadian Supreme Court in *Simon*, Indian treaties are a unique *sui generis* legal interest "which is neither created nor terminated according to the rules of international law."[27] The court took the approach that treaties were to be looked at as being *sui generis* of their own special kind.

2. The Nature of Aboriginal Title

St. Catherine's Milling and Lumber Co. v. The Queen was the leading case on aboriginal title in Canada for more than eighty years. The Judicial Committee of the Privy Council held that aboriginal title over land was recognized only at the Crown's will, and could be taken away at any time.[28] The Privy Council stated that the 1763 Proclamation gave rise to aboriginal title. The Proclamation affirmed and amplified that "the existing treaties and compacts with the Aboriginal nations were sacred and inviolable; that they were binding on the Crown, colonies, and subject; that they were acts of state establishing rights; and that they were enforceable in the courts."[29] In addition, the Proclamation provisioned that the Crown was obligated to deal on Indian's behalf when land was surrendered. It further stipulated that Indians could only surrender their lands to the Crown to prevent exploitations. Based on the Proclamation's framework, *St. Catherine's* case depicted an early picture of the aboriginal title in Canada: 1) the nature of aboriginal interest in land as a personal and usufructuary right that operated as a burden on the

Crown's underlying title; and 2) the right of possession was dependent on the express recognition by the Crown.[30]

In 1973 Canadian Supreme Court revisited the aboriginal title issues in the *Calder* case.[31] It was a split decision, but all six judges agree that aboriginal title exists and is an inherent right capable of recognition by the common law; not dependent on the "good will" of the Crown.[32] Justice Judson, in describing the nature of Indian title, concluded: "The fact in that when the settlers came the Indians were there, organized in societies and occupying the land as their forefathers had done for centuries. This is what Indian title means. What they are asserting in this action is that they had a right to continue to live on their lands as their forefathers had lived and that this right had never been lawfully extinguished."[33] *Calder* represented first modern recognition of aboriginal title in Canadian common law. As the first major court decision of its kind in the Commonwealth, the *Calder* case also set precedents for Australia, New Zealand and many other countries worldwide.

3. The Proof of Aboriginal Title

The inclusion of s.35 of the 1982 Constitution Act signalled a new era of judicial development on the aboriginal title in the Canadian legal regime. The *Guerin* decision of the Supreme Court created and described the duty of the Crown to act as a fiduciary in its dealings with aboriginal peoples.[34] The Court continued to describe the aboriginal title as a unique interest in land "best characterized by its general inalienability, couple with the fact that the Crown is under an obligation to deal with the land on the Indians' behalf when the interest is surrendered."[35] In order to make out a claim for aboriginal title, aboriginal peoples must satisfy the following criteria[36]: 1) organized society, 2) occupation of specific territory, 3) occupation was exclusive, and 4) occupation established at time sovereignty asserted.

On December 11, 1997, the Supreme Court of Canada released its decision in *Delgamuukw v. British Columbia*.[37] The decision marked the first time that the Canadian court had ruled that the concept of aboriginal title exists. The *Delgamuukw* decision did not recognize aboriginal title on any First Nation. It simply outlined a test for proving it. Justice Lamer, on the question of the content of aboriginal title, provided the first, clear, definitive legal definition: "Aboriginal title is a *sui generis* right in land, something between free simple title and a personal and usufructuary right. Aboriginal title is inalienable, except to the Crown. Aboriginal title has its legal source in prior occupation of the land."[38]

The *Delgamuukw* decision recognized that aboriginal land tenure systems have always existed in North America. As Professor James (Sákéj) Henderson commented, "The *Delgamuukw* guidelines affirm and recognize that Aboriginal tenure is *sui generis* tenure: a self-generating system of land tenure protected by section 35 (1) of the Constitution Act, 1982. The sources, content, and meaning of a *sui generis* tenure exist in Aboriginal world-views, languages, laws, perspectives and practices. A *sui generis* tenure does not take its source or meanings from European, British, Canadian law or practice, and exists independently of recognition of the tenure."[39] According to the Lamer Court, aboriginal title is the right to exclusive use and occupation of the land held for a variety of purposes, which need not be aspects of those aboriginal practices, customs and traditions that are integral to distinctive aboriginal cultures, and those protected used must not be irreconcilable with the nature of the group's attachment to that land.[40] It should be noted that aboriginal title is held communally by the aboriginal group and can be transferred, sold or surrendered only to the federal Crown.[41] In order to prove Aboriginal title, First Nations peoples must make a compelling case in each of the following aspects[42]:

a. Land must be occupied prior to sovereignty—the use of land can be proven by actual possession and/ or reliance on the aboriginal society's laws relating to land.
b. There must be continuity between present day and pre-

sovereignty occupation.

c. Occupation must be exclusive, although shared exclusivity is possible.

Delgamuukw was a far-reaching and significant decision in that it paved the way for First Nations of Canada to have their aboriginal title recognized by Canadian courts and legitimized under the Canadian Constitution.

In retrospect, Canadian constitutional law and legal development have been slowly equalizing authority between aboriginal peoples and the colonists. The Supreme Court of Canada has noted that before the constitutional reform of 1982, the courts ignored aboriginal and treaty rights.[43] In the *Reference by the Governor General in Council Concerning Certain Questions Relating to the Secession of Quebec*, [1998] 2 S.C.R. 217, the court commented that the constitutional reforms changed this legal context:

> the explicit protection for existing aboriginal and treaty rights, and in s. 25, a non-derogation clause in favour of the rights of aboriginal peoples. The "promise" of s. 35, as it was termed in *R. v. Sparrow*, [1990] 1 S.C.R. 1075, at p. 1083, recognized not only the ancient occupation of land by aboriginal peoples, but their contribution to the building of Canada, and the special framers of the *Constitution Act, 1982* included in s. 35 commitments made to them by successive governments. The protection of these rights, so recently and arduously achieved, whether looked at in their own right or as part of the larger concern with minorities, reflects an important underlying constitutional value.

Aboriginal interests and customary laws survived the assertion of sovereignty by the Crown, and were elevated to constitutional status by section 35 of the Constitution Act, 1982. Aboriginal rights were constitutionally entrenched but not specified in the Constitution Act of 1982. Section 35 of the Constitution provides:

(1) The existing aboriginal and treaty rights of the aboriginal peoples of Canada are hereby recognized and affirmed.

(2) In this Act, "aboriginal peoples of Canada" includes the Indian, Inuit and Métis peoples of Canada.
(3) For greater certainty, in subsection (1) "treaty rights" includes rights that now exist by way of land claims agreements or may be so acquired.
(4) Notwithstanding any other provision of this Act, the aboriginal and treaty rights referred to in subsection (1) are guaranteed equally to male and female persons.

III. Conclusion—A Pattern of Practice of Aboriginal Title as Indigenous Peoples' Rights to Land Constitutes Customary International Law

Marshall Court of the United States in the early nineteenth century delivered three landmark decisions, which formed the bases of Indian claims of original Indian title and still are most cited cases despite their age.[44] The *Calder* decision of the Canadian Supreme Court represented the first modern recognition of the idea of aboriginal title in the common law. Common law rights arise when facts exist and the Court construed that if these facts exist, then the right exists. That is, if there is aboriginal historic presence on the land, then these rights can be recognized as common law without the need for any action by the government—something called aboriginal title.[45] Aboriginal title was variously described as 'proprietary', 'personal', 'usufructuary', '*sui generis*', and as 'possessory'. More recently it has been described as being a 'bundle of rights.'[46] Perhaps the most fundamental justification for aboriginal rights is that indigenous peoples lived on and occupied the land before the arrival of colonial settlers. A claim of prior occupancy suggests that, all other things being equal, a prior occupant of land possesses a stronger claim to that land than subsequent arrivals.[47] Aboriginal title stems from this prior occupancy. Accordingly, aboriginal title is "a right to the land itself" which is proprietary in nature.[48]

Based on the foregoing demonstrations, Australia, Canada, and the U.S. recognize and affirm indigenous peoples' relationships with the land and its resources. Aboriginal title as indigenous peoples' rights to land creates *sui generis* forms of property within a number of national legal systems.[49] Furthermore, such form of property has been complemented by a number of international instruments to protect aboriginal interests in land over the past two decades. This initiative began with the International Labour Organization's dedications in its two conventions, which expressly safeguard aboriginal title to land. Indigenous peoples' right to the land they traditionally inhabit is recognized in the ILO Convention No. 107 of 1957.[50] Apart from criticisms for its assimilationist approach,[51] Convention 107 was significant because, for the first time as an international institution, it established binding and obligatory standards to protect aboriginal property rights to their traditional lands. Moreover, Convention 107 recognized indigenous peoples' collective land ownership.

Another instrument is the ILO Convention No. 169 of 1989.[52] In Professor Williams' words, it is "international law's most concrete manifestation of the growing recognition of indigenous peoples' rights to property in lands."[53] Detailed provisions made for the protection of aboriginal land rights are framed in Part II of the Convention. In particular, Article 14 (1) reads,

> The rights of ownership and possession of the peoples concerned over the lands which they traditionally occupy shall be recognized. In addition, measures shall be taken inappropriate cases to safeguard the right of the peoples concerned to use lands not exclusively occupied by them, but to which they have traditionally had access for their subsistence and traditional activities. Particular attention shall be paid to the situation of nomadic peoples and shifting cultivators in this respect.

In the inter-American sphere, aboriginal rights to land are strengthened in article 18 of the Proposed American Declaration on the Rights of Indigenous Peoples.[54] Additionally, indigenous peoples have a deep relationship with the land they live in. In this sense, it explains why indigenous property rights to land cannot be separated from their traditional patterns of land tenure.

As the Proposed American Declaration states, Article XVIII, 3 (iii)

> Nothing . . . shall be construed as limiting the right of indigenous peoples to attribute ownership within the community in accordance with their customs, traditions, uses and traditional practices, nor shall it affect any collective community rights over them.

One of the most important international initiatives for indigenous peoples is the U.N. Declaration on the Rights of Indigenous Peoples,[55] which provides further evidence of the increasingly international recognition of indigenous peoples' property rights in lands. Article 26 of the Declaration reads,

> Indigenous peoples have the right to own, develop, control and use the lands and territories, including the total environment of the lands, air, waters, coastal seas, sea-ice, flora and fauna and other resources which they have traditionally owned or otherwise occupied or used. This includes the right to the full recognition of their laws, traditions and customs, land-tenure systems and institutions for the development and management of resources, and the right to effective measures by States to prevent any interference with, alienation of or encroachment upon these rights.

Aboriginal title as indigenous peoples' rights to land is inextricably interconnected with international instruments. We can observe a pattern of activity by U.N. bodies and other international organizations, such as the OAS, in conjunction with numerous state practices. According to Professor Williams, "The international norms that recognize rights based on indigenous peoples' traditional landholdings and resource use are increasingly incorporated and reflected in the domestic legal practice of states throughout the American region and the world."[56] These activities demonstrate a steadily broadening consensus that aboriginal title is a rule of customary international law.[57]

NOTES

1. Joy Harjo, *Secrets from the Centre of World* (Tucson: University of Arizona Press, 1989).
2. David J. Hayton, *Megarry's Manual of the Law of Real Property* (London: Stevens, 6th ed., 1982). He states "The basis of English land law is that all land in England is owned by the Crown. A small part is in the actual occupation of the Crown; the rest is occupied by tenants holding either directly or indirectly from the Crown."
3. James (Sákéj) Youngblood Henderson, et al., *Aboriginal Tenure in the Constitution of Canada* (Scarborough, ON: Carswell, 2000).
4. Article 91 of the Canadian Constitution Act, 1867.
5. Canadian law acknowledges the legal significance of the fact that aboriginal people occupied the continent from 'time immemorial.' See *Calder v. A.G.B.C.*, [1973] S.C.R. 313 at 368, per Hall J., dissenting on other grounds.
6. As Professor Singer points out, "Once the State obtained title from the relevant Indian nation, the federal government then granted patents (titles) to the land to individuals, corporations and state government. Non-Indian titles therefore generally derive not from first possession, but from "state grant" by the federal government." For further discussions, see Joseph William Singer, *Introduction to Property* (New York: Aspen Law & Business, 2001), 705.
7. James Tully, *Aboriginal Property and Western Theory: Recovering a Middle Ground*, in Ellen Frankel Paul, Fred. D. Miller, Jr., and Jeffrey Paul, ed., *Property Rights* (Cambridge: Cambridge University Press, 1994), 158-69.
8. Francisco de Vitoria, *Francisco de Vitoria De Indis et De ivre belli relections*, ed. Ernest Nys (Washington: The Carnegie Institution of Washington, 1917), 137-39.
9. *Id.* at 129.
10. *Id.* at 120-23.
11. *Id.* at 127-28. Vitoria's work demonstrated that indigenous peoples were viewed as early as 1630s as the absolute and true owners of the continent, and as such were empowered to retain title to their lands.

12. Felix S. Cohen, *Original Indian Title*, 32 Minn. L. Rev. 28, 43-44 (1947). Cohen contended that "our concepts of Indian title . . . are to be traced to Spanish origins, and particularly to doctrines developed by Francisco de Vitoria, the real founder of modern international law."
13. Vine Deloria, Jr. & Clifford M. Lytle, *American Indians, American Justice* 2-6 (Austin: University of Texas Press, 1983).
14. Robert A. Williams, Jr., *The American Indian in Western Legal Thought: The Discourses of Conquest* (New York: Oxford University Press, 1990), 96-107.
15. James (Sákéj) Youngblood Henderson et al., 5-6.
16. Kent McNeil, *Common Law Aboriginal Title* (Oxford: Clarendon Press, 1989).
17. John J. Borrows & Leonard I. Rotman, *Aboriginal Legal Issues: Cases, Materials & Commentary* (Toronto: Butterworths, 1998), 4-11.
18. Robert Odawi Porter, compiler, *Sovereignty, Colonialism and The Indigenous Nations* (Durham, N.C.: Carolina Academic Press, 2005).
19. Paul G. McHugh, *Aboriginal Societies and the Common Law: A History of Sovereignty, Status, and Self-Determination* (New York: Oxford University Press, 2004), 45. According to McHugh, "it [the Royal Proclamation] was a pan-colonial statement for the settlers' information and benefit of a uniform basis for the exercise of the Crown's discretionary authority relating to dealings with the Indians and land title."
20. *Id.* at 45. McHugh observed, "Governors of British North America in the period before the Quebec Act (1774) were to take 'effective Care' in their application of the Proclamation. They were told also 'to cultivate and maintain a strict Friendship and good Correspondence' with the neighbouring tribes and 'to Use the best means You can for Conciliating their Affections and Uniting them to Our Government'."
21. Royal Proclamation of 1763, cited Robert A. Williams, Jr., 237.
22. McHugh, *supra* note 19, at 104-105.
23. John Borrows, *Recovering Canada: The Resurgence of Indigenous Law* (Toronto: University of Toronto Press, 2002), 125-27.

24. John Borrows, *Wampum at Niagara: The Royal Proclamation, Canadian Legal History and Self-Government*, in Michael Asch, ed., *Aboriginal and Treaty Rights in Canada: Essay on Law, Equality and Respect for Difference* (Vancouver: U.B.C. Press, 1997), 168-69.
25. *Id.* (The idea of selling land in an English concept had no equivalent in many Aboriginal communities. Entering into a kinship relationship where the English could use the lands as their needs arose without interfering with the Aboriginal nations' own needs would be more likely to be the understanding of the Aboriginal nation. Also, respectful sharing of the land would have been understood. Thirdly, allies in time of war against common enemies would have been understood. Lastly, provision of aide to one another when the other couldn't manage would have been understood.)
26. Borrows & Rotman, *supra* note 17, at 105-8. See also *Simon v. The Queen*, [1985] 2 S.C.R. 387.
27. *Simon v. The Queen*, [1985] 2 S.C.R. 387. The Court concluded, "While it may be helpful in some instances to analogize the principles of international treaty law to Indian treaties, these principles are not determinative. An Indian treaty is unique; it is an agreement *sui generis* which is neither created nor terminated according to the rules of international law."
28. *St. Catherine's Milling and Lumber Company v. The Queen*, (1887) 14 AC 46; 2 CNLC 541, 545.
29. *Vajesingji Jaoravarsingji v. Secretary of State for India in Council* (1924), 51 L.R. Ind. App. 357, Lord Dunedin, citing *Cook v. Sprigg*, [1899] A.C. 572 (P.C.)
30. *St. Catherine's Milling*, *supra* note 28. (The original aboriginal inhabitants who had been living on the land from time immemorial were found to have no real property interest in the land at all; rather, they had a mere 'personal' and 'usufructuary' right that constituted a burden on the Crown's otherwise absolute title. Moreover, Lord Watson attributed the Indian interest solely to the provisions of the *Royal Proclamation of 1763*, equating it with a grant from the Crown.)
31. *Calder v. Attorney General of British Columbia*, [1973] 34 D.L.R. (3d) 145 (S.C.C.).

32. *Id.* (Justice Wilfred Judson, speaking for three judges, found that the Nisgaá, before the coming of the white man, had aboriginal title, a title recognized under English law. But, he went on to say, this title had been implicitly extinguished by pre-Confederation enactments of the old colony British Columbia. On the other hand, Justice Emmett Hall, speaking for three judges, found that Nisgaá aboriginal title had never been lawfully extinguished, and that this title could be asserted even today.)
33. *Id.*
34. *Guerin et al v. The Queen*, [1984] 2 S.C.R. 335.
35. *Id.*
36. *Hamlet of Baker Lake v. Minister of Indian Affairs*, [1980] 1 FC 518 (FCTD).
37. *Delgamuukw v. British Columbia*, [1997] 3 S.C.R. 1010.
38. *Id.*
39. James (Sákéj) Youngblood Henderson, *The Impact of Delgamuukw Guidelines in Atlantic Canada*, in Owen Lippert, ed., *Beyond the Nass Valley: National Implications of the Supreme Court's Delgamuukw Decision* (Vancouver: The Fraser Institute, 2000).
40. *Delgamuukw v. British Columbia*, [1997] 3 S.C.R. 1010. ("Constitutionally recognized aboriginal rights fall along a spectrum with respect to their degree of connection with the land. At the one end are those aboriginal rights which are practices, customs and traditions integral to the distinctive aboriginal culture of the group claiming the right but where the use and occupation of the land where the activity is taking place is not sufficient to support a claim of title to the land. In the middle are activities which, out of necessity, take place on land and indeed, might be intimately related to a particular piece of land. Although an aboriginal group may not be able to demonstrate title to the land, it may nevertheless have a site-specific right to engage in a particular activity. At the other end of the spectrum is aboriginal title itself which confers more than the right to engage in site-specific activities which are aspects of the practices, customs and traditions of distinctive aboriginal cultures. Site-specific rights can be made out even if title cannot. Because aboriginal rights can vary with respect to their degree of connection with the land, some aboriginal groups may be unable to make out a claim to title, but will nevertheless possess

aboriginal rights that are recognized and affirmed by s. 35 (1), including site-specific rights to engage in particular activities.")

41. *Id.*
42. *Id.*
43. *R. v. Sparrow*, [1990] 1 S.C.R. 1075.
44. These three cases, also known as 'Marshall Trilogy', established the foundations for the development of U.S. Federal Indian Law and Policy. See *Johnson v. McIntosh*, 21 U.S. (8 Wheat) 543 (1823); *Worcester v. Georgia*, 31 US (6 Pet.) 515 (1832); and *Cherokee Nation v. Georgia*, 30 U.S. 1 (1831). The Cherokee Nation invoked the Supreme Court's original jurisdiction to enjoin on the State of Georgia's laws prohibiting implementation of certain laws of that state on the Cherokee Nation reservation. Pursuant to the Constitution, all regulations concerning commerce with Indian nations were within the sole power of the federal government. In what is known as the Commerce Clause, the founding Fathers empowered Congress to "regulate commerce with foreign nations, and among the several states, and with the Indian tribes (U.S. Constitution, Article I, Section 8, clause 3)." The Supreme Court was authorized to hear only matters of "original jurisdiction," that is, matters expressly provided for in the Constitution. The Supreme Court held that the Cherokee Nation was not a foreign nation, rather a "domestic dependent nation" subject to the sovereignty of the U.S. federal government. Since the tribe was neither a "state" nor a "foreign nation," the Supreme Court held that the motion for an injunction was not a matter of original jurisdiction and refused to grant the injunction. For detailed discussions, see Robert T. Anderson et al., ed., *Cohen's Handbook of Federal Indian Law* (Albuquerque, N.M.: American Indian Law Centre, 2005).
45. *Calder*, *supra* note 31.
46. Federal Court of Australia, [2000] FCA 191, *The State of Western Australia & ORS v. Ben Ward & ORS*. The court defined native title as follows: a) A right to possess, occupy, use and enjoy the land; b) A right to make decisions about the use and enjoyment of the land; c) A right of access to the land; d) A right to use and enjoy the traditional resources of the land; e) A right to maintain and protect places of importance under traditional laws, customs and practices in the determination area.

47. Patrick Macklem, *Indigenous Difference and the Constitution of Canada* (Toronto: University of Toronto Press, 2001), 78.
48. *Delgamuukw v. British Columbia*, [1998] 1 C.N.L.R. 14 (S.C.C.).
49. *Guerin, supra* note 34. (It is true that the *sui generis* interest which the Indians have in the land is personal in the sense that it cannot be transferred to a grantee, but it is also true that the interest gives rise upon surrender to a distinctive fiduciary obligation on the part of the Crown to deal with the land for the benefit of surrendering Indians.) *Mabo v. Queensland* (No. 2), (1992) 175 CLR 1. (Native title has its origin in and is given its content by the traditional customs observed by the indigenous inhabitants of a territory. The nature and incidents of native title must be ascertained as a matter of fact by reference to those laws and customs.) *Begay v. Keedah*, 19 Indian L. Rep. 6021 (Navajo Supreme Court 1991). (Traditional Navajo land tenure is not the same as English common law tenure, as used in the United States. Navajo have always occupied land in family units, using the land for subsistence. Families and subsistence residential units (as they are sometimes called) hold land in a form of communal ownership.)
50. ILO Convention No. 107 Concerning the Protection and Integration of Indigenous and Other Tribal and Semi-Tribal Populations in Independent Countries, adopted on June 26 1957, International Labour Conference, 328 U.N.T.S. 247 (entered into force on June 2 1959). Article 11, "The right of ownership, collective or individual, of the members of populations concerned over the lands which these populations traditionally occupy shall be recognized."
51. S. James Anaya, *Indigenous Peoples in International Law* (New York: Oxford University Press, 2nd ed., 2004), 55-56, 58.
52. ILO Convention Concerning Indigenous and Tribal Peoples in Independent Countries (Convention No. 169), June 27, 1989, International Labour Conference, 28 I.L.M. 1382 (entered into force September 5, 1991).
53. Robert A. Williams, Jr., *Amicus Curiae Brief* (presented by the National Congress of American Indians in the case of the Mayagna (Sumo) Community of Awas Tingni), Inter-American Court of Human Rights Case No. 11.577.
54. Proposed American Declaration on the Rights of Indigenous Peoples, approved by the Inter-American Commission on Human

Rights 26 February 1997, at its 1333rd session, 95th regular session. The Proposed American Declaration is currently undergoing further examination at the request of the OAS General Assembly. Article XVIII, "1. Indigenous peoples have the right to the legal recognition of their varied and specific forms and modalities of their control, ownership, use and enjoyment of territories and property. 2. Indigenous peoples have the right to the recognition of their property and ownership rights with respect to lands, territories and resources they have historically occupied, as well as to the use of those to which they have historically had access for their traditional activities and livelihood."

55. Human Rights Council Resolution 2006/2, *Working Group of the Commission on Human Rights to elaborate a draft declaration in accordance with paragraph 5 of the General Assembly resolution 49/214 of 23 December 1994*, 29 June 2006.
56. Williams, *supra* note 53.
57. Siegfried Wiessner, *Rights and Status of Indigenous Peoples: A Global Comparative and International Legal Analysis*, 12 Harv. Hum. Rts. J. 57, (1999), 109. As Professor Wiessner concludes, "Today, many of these proposed or actual prescriptions, coinciding, as they do, with domestic state practice . . . have created a new set of shared expectations about the legal status and rights of indigenous peoples that has matured and crystallized into customary international law."

“Lost” Children: Crossing Indigenous Cultural Borders in the Canadian Arctic

KIMBERLEY MCMAHON-COLEMAN
University of Wollongong, Australia

This paper focuses on artistic representations of the cultural loss faced by Indigenous children when removed from their traditional lands and homes. It frames the mission project in Canada as being an integral part of the assimilation process, and one which effectively produced diasporic sensibilities within Indigenous cultural groups, and is part of a wider project which compares the Inuit experience with those of the Australian Murri from Queensland. Key tools of assimilationist agendas included evangelism, the loss of traditional languages and the removal of children from their families and traditional lands. These are also key features of genocide as defined by the United Nations in 1948 (Armitage 6), as well as by-products of residential schooling programs. They are also significant contributing factors in the lives of the Inuit artists whose work is examined here.

Although the concept of Indigenous diaspora may at first glance appear to be a contradiction in terms, it is well established that notions of the uncanny and home are central to literature in postcolonial cultures, because uncanny experiences are those which happen when “one’s home is rendered, somehow and in some sense, unfamiliar; one has the experience, in other words, of being in place and out of place simultaneously” (Gelder and Jacobs 23). Historically, this was a common experience among those first moving to the colonies, and it was certainly the experience of Indigenous subjects in the nations which were colonised.

The colonisation of the Inuit shared many facets of the concerted subjugation of Indigenous peoples elsewhere. Canadian history, like that of Australia and numerous other settler-colonies, featured an attempt to eradicate Indigenous spirituality and language, in part through the use of residential and billeted schooling systems. First Nations and Inuit children were systematically removed from their families and traditional lands and relocated in southern cities. Residential schools were often administered by churches, and endeavoured to "reprogram" Indigenous children, teaching them the English language and "Christian values" with trademark missionary zeal. The program was still in place as recently as the 1970s, and high unemployment rates in the Arctic in the intervening decades have led to the continued migration south of Inuit youth. This movement across traditional borders has created a kind of intra-national diasporic condition, which the Inuit continue to negotiate on a daily basis. As a result, the work of a number of Inuit artists makes use of the motif of the "Lost Child," and the isolation of a young person in the cities of the South. Filmmaker Elisapie Isaac, sculptor David-Ruben Piqtoukun and the late artist, writer and cartoonist Alootook Ipellie, have all made use of this idea in their works.

From the times of earliest contact with Europeans, there have been incidents involving the removal of Inuit from the Arctic; firstly for display purposes, and later as a means of "civilizing" that society. The first recorded such incident occurred in 1567 when an Inuk woman and her daughter were captured by French sailors who had murdered her husband during a confrontation on the Labrador coast, and were subsequently presented as live curios in Antwerp and at the Augsburg Fair (d'Anglure 205). A woodcut of the mother and child, completed in Augsberg at this time and entitled "Portrait of savages," is the earliest known European artistic representation of the Inuit.

In other cases, the issue of Inuit consenting or otherwise to travel to Europe has been much more complicated. The display of Inuit in zoos and other exhibitions, and their conversion to Christianity, would converge in *The Diary of Abraham Ulrikab* (2005), which is widely regarded as the first example of Inuit autobiography.[1] It tells the story of a group of Inuit who were displayed at Hagenbeck's Zoo in Hamburg in 1880, and later in Prague, Frankfurt, Darstadt and Paris (Lutz, xxiii-xxiv). Although the co-option of Abraham by recruiter Adrian Jacobsen of Hagenbeck's company could hardly be described as a kidnap, the Inuk's financial circumstances meant that he had limited choices available to him. In correspondence included in the volume, a Moravian missionary, Brother Kretschmer, noted that Abraham and his family had "suffered great poverty" the previous year, yet had been too proud to accept assistance from the alms box (Lutz 10). The opportunity for both himself and other members of his family to earn regular money must have seemed an answer to the neophyte Christian's prayers. Unfortunately this expedition would not be as successful as Jacobsen's previous, Inuit display venture, some three years previously. In this instance, Jacobsen was hospitalised, delaying the vaccination of his Inuit charges. It was to be a fatal error; all eight Inuit on the trip died of smallpox within weeks of arriving in Europe (Lutz xix-xx).

In an echo of the complicated politics around whether these removals from home and culture were directly or indirectly coerced, the legacies of the policies of enforced removal of children to residential schools even after the programs were radically modified. According to John Milloy in his work *A National Crime,* in the post-residential schooling era, children considered to be "at risk" in the opinions of Euro-Canadian teachers, clergy or public servants, were often still placed in the institutions, which became part of the welfare system (Milloy 211). Others, like Ipellie, were fostered by white families in the south. In later years, young Inuit like Elisapie Isaac would have access to secondary schooling without leaving their homes and families, but the limited employment opportunities in the Arctic environment would mean that exile from their homelands eventually became a financial necessity.

Isaac's contemporaries, like members of earlier generations who were forcibly removed from their families under the residential schooling system, have become part of an Indigenous Diaspora; never truly at home in their host communities, nor able to completely return to their homelands. Diasporans are typically forced from their homes, but equally, may be coerced to leave when social, political and economic circumstances mean that it is no longer viable to stay there. As Noelene Brasche has argued, the forced displacement of Indigenous peoples "infringed traditional boundaries. . . . Territorial or national groups who previously had little or nothing in common now shared experiences of dispersal and loss of sovereignty, as well as physical displacement from traditional country" (Brasche 49). William Safran, a pioneer of diaspora studies, defines diasporic communities as those that have been displaced from a specific original location to two or more peripheral regions; retain a collective memory; feel partly isolated and insulated from their host society; regard their ancestral home as their true home and a place to which they or their descendants would like to return; are committed to the maintenance or restoration of their homeland, and that they continue to relate personally or vicariously to their homeland (Safran 83). Clearly, these indicators are all features of the modern Inuit experience.

Issues surrounding home and identity are as pertinent to Indigenous people removed from their families and familial settings as they are to people who have crossed national borders. Robin Cohen has defined the trauma of banishment in diasporic communities as being typified by "dream[ing] of home but liv[ing] in exile,' (Cohen ix) factors which are clearly evident in the indigenous experience of social, cultural, and linguistic displacement. Certainly two conflicting cultures influence the daily lives of these people, so that issues relating to identity and belonging remain contentious.

Diasporic literature and art are fundamentally concerned with notions of home, exile and belonging. When I first visited Ottawa in May 2004, I was shown a sculpture installed outside the Ottawa City Hall—"The Lost Child," by an Inuk artist, David-Ruben Piqtoukun. A plaque explains that the sandstone piece was inspired by the artist's removal to a residential school in Edmonton as a five-year-old, and his feelings of loneliness and isolation beneath an "overwhelming urban skyline." Of this time, he has said, "I . . . lost speaking my language, and Native Eskimo ways. Living in the south, it made my identity more difficult to comprehend. I was 'lost between two worlds.'" The plaque's final line reflects the artist's belief that "we have all been lost at some point in our lives." For Piqtoukun, using the traditional medium of stone carving, which he began to learn at the age of 22, has helped him regain a sense of ritual and culture. He says, "[m]y Inuit culture is rich again in many ways and I feel rich in spirit for having continued to explore images in stone" (Canada House Gallery 1-2).

The guide who introduced me to this sculpture was Alootook Ipellie, an Inuk artist, cartoonist, writer and poet. Born in a hunting camp called Nuvuqquq on Baffin Island, then known as Frobisher Bay, in 1951, he and his family abandoned their semi-nomadic lifestyle and moved into the township of Iqaluit when he was four, as part of a government-funded program to move the nomadic Inuit into settlements. Shortly after his fifth birthday, he was removed to the Mountain Sanatorium in Hamilton, Ontario, for tuberculosis treatment. When he was returned almost a year later, he was more fluent in English than in his native Inuktitut. Despite this, however, he notes in the introduction to *Arctic Dreams and Nightmares* that it was not until he was removed to the Ottawa for secondary schooling in 1967 that he felt he was no longer an "Innumarik"—a real Inuk (vii). He boarded with a white Euro-Canadian family, and was expected to speak English and attend a comprehensive high school. The culture shock that he experienced as a result was acute, and continued to inform his work until his sudden death in 2007. Although he lived and worked in Ottawa for four decades, he longed to return to the Arctic, which he called his spiritual home. As he explained,

> my mind, my psyche, is at home up in the Arctic, and it will always be that way. And I'm thinking one day I'll go back to my real home. (McMahon-Coleman 77)

This idea of living between two worlds is clearly evident in his work. In particular, Ipellie is critical of the evangelical process which was a key feature of Canada's assimilationist Indigenous policies. Victor Ramraj has argued that diasporans are [c]aught psychically between two worlds" (Ramraj 216), and this is evident in the bicultural spirituality of the characters in Ipellie's work. Ipellie, who often refers to his grandfather Inutsiaq, as his anchor, saw him as emblematic of the colonial influence on Inuit spirituality. Inutsiaq was a shaman, and the young Alootook was identified as having the potential to also become an *angakkuq* or shaman. Typically, the development of shamanistic power in such children was developed by the elders of the community (Bennett & Rowley 2004), but Inutsiaq converted to Christianity when Alootook was still a small child. From his childhood onwards, then, he felt a sense of lost opportunity and heritage.

As Jim Miller has noted, the early days of colonialism involved competition among shamans and priests for the souls of Indigenous peoples (Miller 53), a conflict which Ipellie explores in a number of his short stories, including "The Exorcism," and "I, Crucified," which were both published in his 1993 illustrated collection, *Arctic Dreams and Nightmares.* "The Exorcism" depicts a battle between two shamans, one of whom is named "Guti," the Inuktitut word for God, and Kappia, meaning "Sacred," who represents traditional Inuit spirituality. "I, Crucified" tells the story of a shaman who finds himself crucified on the tundra, nailed to a whalebone cross by jealous competitors. Both stories make clear the deeply-held suspicion of Christianity which permeates Ipellie's work, yet draws on the iconography of the imported religion. As Austin & Scott argue in *Canadian Missionaries, Indigenous Peoples: Representing Religion at Home and Abroad,*

> [i]n embracing Christianity, Aboriginal people did not entirely forsake connections to their heritage, land, or indigenous cultural expressions. . . . This self identification is a shifting one, and not the sole reference point for the individual. (101)

Another of Ipellie's key concerns as a result of his own diasporic experience was that of the education of young Inuit. Ipellie was vocal in his support of educational programs which teach children in Inuktitut. Ulf Hannerz argues in *Transnational Connections: Culture, People, Places* that beneath the guise of philanthropy, the removal of children from their families and cultures in the name of education had a more sinister outcome; that of teaching Indigenous children their 'place' in society.

> Education creates difference, as it sorts and prepares people for that division of knowledge which matches a contemporary division of labour . . . the state comes in at an early point in the overall formation of the cultural continuum. . . . In supplying people with different amounts of educational assets, in promoting an organization of the division of labour to no small extent around this distribution, and in thereby giving its support to one principle of cultural as well as social hierarchy, the state opens up that space to transnational influences at one end, and indicates a direction for internal processes. (71-73)

Ipellie's place in the "cultural continuum" was clearly marked, and as he wryly noted, as a "failure in academics, [he] was a perfect candidate to also be a failure in the job market" (A. Ipellie, *People II* 27). He remained critical of an education system which failed to teach students in their native tongue. As he noted during our interview of October 2005,

> when I was a little kid in Iqaluit, we started going to school, we weren't taught anything. I mean in Inuktitut. We had English teachers. No one taught us anything about our own culture, our own language, our heritage. The only reason why I learnt anything about us, about Inuit, was by being with my family on the land. And also, I learned how to read and write Inuktitut syllabics in Sunday school. In those days, the school wasn't involved (McMahon-Coleman *ACS*).

His cartoon below depicts education as a battleground, and hints at the violent history of residential systems and its historical successors.

"Who Teaches the Child?" *Inuit Monthly,* Vol. 4, No. 3: 69

Milloy has noted elsewhere the irony of behind the stated protective and evangelical missions of the residential schools; that the children

> came, or, more accurately, were taken, from their parents and communities, and they suffered; the system did not provide . . . the education . . . that was the promise of Christ's call, 'Come unto me.' Instead, the system's history is marked by the persistent ne-

> glect and abuse of children and through them of Aboriginal communities in general. (Milloy xiii)

There is currently a movement within Nunavut to translate teaching texts into Inuktitut, and every year interns trained in Ottawa return to the Arctic to teach young people in their own language. This is itself, of course, ironic; in order to gain teaching qualifications, young Inuit are required to head South, because there is still insufficient educational access in Nunavut. This continued movement to Southern Canada because of limited opportunities in the Arctic was the focus of Elisapie Isaac's award-winning directorial debut, *If the Weather Permits.* Born in 1978 to an Inuk mother and a Newfoundlander father who was working for the Hudsons Bay Company, she grew up in Salluit with an adoptive Inuit family. The film was written as though it was a letter to her late grandfather, as Isaac returns to her homeland and questions how Inuit culture can survive in the modern world. In her voice-over narration, Isaac notes that as a young person, she "felt the need to leave. The immensity of the land and ice oppressed. I took the risk of getting lost in order to find myself" (Isaac).

In 1999 she moved to Montreal and began studying communications at St John's College. A number of members of her immediate family, including her adoptive mother, birth mother and grandfather died in close succession, and she notes that she felt

> lost in the chaos of Montreal. And the spirit of the elders began inhabiting my silences. . . . Since your deaths, since I left Salluit, I've been afraid of fading away. (Isaac)

In 2001 she won a bursary designed to encourage young Indigenous filmmakers to produce their own movies, which enabled her to return to Salluit and explore the twin legacies of traditional Inuit culture and white colonialism. In the short film, which won the Rigoberta Menchu Tum Grand Prize for the First Peoples' Festival in 2003, she interviews young people from Salluit, who appear to have embraced mainstream culture. She asks them about their Christian beliefs, and finds that they believe wholly in heaven and hell. One of them says adamantly, "I don't want to be a shaman. I don't want to go to hell." The young men are distinctly uneasy when she asks them where their shamanic ancestors went after death. They all express a desire to head south, and when asked what they'd like to see in their hometown, one remarks, "A road to other villages would be nice," to which his friend replies, "A road to anywhere." Throughout the film, Isaac addresses her grandfather, who had been an influential figure during her childhood. This sense of her own youthfulness and conflicting feelings about belonging is further developed through the use of a still photograph of herself as a child, and through footage of her young son, named Ittuq after her grandfather, playing on her grandfather's boat and in the local cemetery. The filmmaker appears to be hoping not only for some resolution to the question of where she belongs, but also that her heritage not be lost to her own child.

Ultimately Isaac herself returns to her life in Montreal, but says that like her hunter grandfather, she "follow[s her own] instincts." In an interview published in *Nunatsiaq News* in 2003, she says that she wanted

> [t]o stand up and say I am Inuit but this is who I am and how I want to go about my future and our future . . . I came back knowing much more about who I am. (Nelson 2)

These three Inuit artists use the motif of the "lost" child to express this sense of cultural alienation since white colonization of the Arctic. Through different media they explore the legacy of the residential schooling system, past Christian evangelical policies, and what it means to be a Canadian Inuk in an increasingly globalised society.

Bibliography

Armitage, Andrew. *Comparing the Policy of Aboriginal Assimilation in Australia, Canada and New Zealand.* Vancouver: University of Vancouver Press, 1998

Austin, Alvin, and Jamie S Scott. *Canadian Missionaries: Indigenous Peoples: Representing Religion at Home and Abroad.* Toronto: University of Toronto Press, 2005.

Bennett, John & Susan Rowley, ed. *Uqalurait: An Oral History of Nunavut.* Montreal & Kingston: McGill-Queen's University Press, 2004

Brasche, Noelene. (2002). *Leaving Country without Leaving the Country.* Sydney University. (Unpublished Thesis).

Canada House Gallery. *David Ruben Piqtoukun.* Google. Online. Accessed April 7, 2005. Available http: //canadahouse,com/dynamic/artists/David_Ruben_Piqtoukun.asp

Cohen, Robin. *Global Diasporas: an Introduction.* London: UCL Press, 1997.

d'Anglure, Bernard Saladin. "Ethnographic Commentary" in *Atanarjuat: the fast runner.* Screenplay by Paul Apak Angilirq. Additional writers: Zacharias Kunuk, Herve Paniaq and Pauloosie Quilitalik. English screenplay by Norman Cohn. Coach House Books, 2002.

Gallagher, Chris & Meagan Dallimore, ed., "International Film Fetsival," *Latitudes,* Issue No. 5, March 2005.

Gelder, Ken and Jane M. Jacobs. *Uncanny Australia: Sacredness and Identity in a Postcolonial Nation.* Carlton South: Melbourne UP, 1998.

Isaac, Elisapie, Dir. *If the Weather Permits.* National Film Board of Canada, 2003.

Ipellie, Alootook. *Arctic Dreams and Nightmares.* Penicton: Theytus, 1993.

——. "Nunatsiaqmiut, People of the Good Land: Part 2," *Inuit Art Quarterly*, (Summer-Fall 1992b): 22-28.

Lutz, Hartmut, Trans. Alootook Ipellie & Hans-Ludwig Blohm. *The Diary of Abraham Ulrikab.* Ottawa: University of Ottawa Press, 2005.

McMahon-Coleman, Kimberley. "Interview with Alootook Ipellie." *Australasian-Canadian Studies—Minorities and Cultural Assertions.* Vol. 23, No. 2, 2005. pp. 77-89.

Merkur, Daniel. *Powers Which We Do Not Know: The Gods and Spirits of the Inuit.* Idaho: Idaho University Press, 1991.

Miller, J.R. *Skyscrapers Hide the Heavens—A History of Indian-White Relations in Canada.* Toronto: University of Toronto Press, 1989. Revised Edition 1991.

Milloy, John S. *A National Crime—the Canadian Government and the Residential School System 1879 to 1986.* Manitoba: University of Manitoba Press, Manitoba Studies in Native History, XI, 1999.

Nelson, Odile. "Salluit performer basks in summer successes." *Nunatsiaq News.* Google. Online. First published August 1, 2003. Accessed April 6, 2006. Available http: //www.nunatsiaq.com/ archives/30801/news/nunavik/ 30801_01.html

Piqtoukun, David-Ruben. "The Lost Child" sculpture. Installation outside Ottawa City Hall, 1989.

Ramraj, Victor J, "Diasporas and Multiculturalism" in Bruce King, ed. *New National & Post-Colonial Literatures: An Introduction.* Oxford: Clarendon Press, 1996. Chapter 12; pp. 214-29.

A Study of Japan's Pre-War Economic Research on Canada: An Analysis of the Japan's Consular Reports

KOJI UTSUNOMIYA
Tezukayama University, Nara, Japan

1. Introduction

The aim of this study is to examine Japan's trade with Canada during the pre-war period. Special attention is paid upon such issues as construction of informational infrastructure to collect and disseminate overseas commercial information and the trade strategy to promote the Japanese primary and secondary goods into Canadian market, mainly based on extensive examination of pre-war Japanese consular reports regarding economic conditions in Canada.

The consular reports from foreign countries were the most valuable for Japanese merchants in the early stages of industrialization, because they had never engaged in overseas trade before, and were eager to have information about foreign markets. Therefore, to assess Canada's role in Japan's world-wide economy after the Meiji Restoration of 1868, it is essential to investigate how and why Japan's economic relations with Canada developed in the past, and when and where they did, in order to consider what kind of relations Japan should construct with Canada in the foreseeable future.

This study focuses on the development of economic relations between Japan and Canada before the First World War, in particular the Meiji era. The order of my discussion is as follows: first, when Japan's economic interests in Canada emerged; second, how economic information was collected from Canada and disseminated among Japanese middlemen and manufacturers; third, the extent to which Japan's trade and commercial networks with Canada developed; and finally, the kind of issues which arose out of its development.

2. A Brief Survey of Commercial Information in Japanese Consular Reports Regarding Canada

Japan's survival as a latecomer capitalist nation depended upon the development of an institutionalized system for the collection and dissemination of commercial information. In order to collect overseas commercial information, the Ministry of Foreign Affairs (MOFA) founded the Consulate System and the Consular Reporting System. The Ministry of Agriculture and Commerce (MOAC) also opened the Overseas Commercial Museums and dispatched Overseas Business Trainees as well (Tsunoyama, 1986; Sugihara, 1996). Economic information regarding Canada was collected through these international networks of information collection, which the Meiji Government had assiduously established with great cost .

Japanese consular reports were printed and published to make their information available to merchants and businesspersons by the Ministry of Foreign Affairs from 1881 to 1943. The title of the periodicals in which these reports' appearance changed frequently, and difficulties arose when one attempts to assemble them into a complete series for study. Table 1 shows that the trade journals included Japanese Consular Reports.

Table 1 Trade Journal included Japanese Consular Reports

Title	Period	Frequency
1. Report of Commerce	1881-1886 (Meiji 14-19)	Semi-annually
2. Commercial Reports	1886/12-1889/12 (Meiji 19-22)	Every three months
3. Official Gazette	1890/12-1905/12 (Meiji 23-33)	Daily
4. Journal of Commercial Reports	1894/1-1913/3 (Meiji 27-	Monthly

	Taisho 2)	
5. *Official Commercial Reports*	1913/4-1924/12 (Taisho 2-13)	Twice a week
6. *Daily Overseas Commercial Reports*	1925/1-1928/3 (Taisho 14-Showa 3)	Daily
7. *Weekly Overseas Economic Conditions*	1928/4-1934/12 (Showa 3-9)	Every Monday
8. *Overseas Economic Conditions*	1935/1-1943/10 (Showa 10-13)	Twice a month

Source: Tsunoyama (1986) and Kitagawa (1997)

In the period of the *Report of Commerce* (1881-1886), information regarding Canada was sent from Japanese consuls in the London or San Francisco. The information collected in these series was all concerning the Canadian Pacific Railway Company (CPR); the freight rate, the commercial conditions and the mail contract between CPR and the United Kingdom in 1889, the opening of the shipping lines between Vancouver and Hong Kong. It was the completion and the development of the CPR that encouraged as a first factor Japan's Consulate to be set up in Canada.

In the period of the *Commercial Reports* (1886/12-1889/12), information regarding Canada was sent from Japanese consuls in New York, San Francisco, Lyon and Vancouver. The information covered the general trend of foreign trade in Canada, the commercial conditions in the Province of British Columbia (BC), the growth of coal industry in BC, the general conditions concerning commerce, agriculture and industries in BC, the names of merchants handling Japanese goods in Vancouver as well as the commercial conditions concerning the CPR. The number of consular reports regarding Canada had risen between 5 in the *Report of Commerce* to 24 in the *Commercial Reports*, but much attention was paid on the economic conditions concerning BC, especially Vancouver. Domestic merchants and manufacturers in Japan had not yet obtained the detailed information on market performance and in Canada East.

In the period of the *Official Gazette* (1890/1-1905/12), the topics were: the trends of Japanese trade with Canada; the commercial conditions in BC and in Vancouver; the opening and the development of shipping lines between Canada and Australia; the effect of the amendment of the tariff system in Canada on the demand for Japanese goods; the development of salmon canning industry of the Fraser river; the research on the demand of Japanese silk piece goods and rice; and so on. These pieces of information regarding Canada were sent from Japanese consuls in New York, San Francisco, Honolulu and Vancouver.

Thereafter in the age of the *Journal of Commercial Reports* (1894/1-1913/3), reports on Canada increased substantially on such matters of concern to Japan as Canadian industrial policy, the anti-Japanese movement, British commercial policy to the cotton cloth market, the United States commercial policy to the cotton piece goods market, the report of the Mission to East Canada, the trends of Japanese trade with Canada, the commercial conditions in BC and Vancouver (especially lumber, coal, pulp, salmon, and gold mining industries), the sales campaign of Japanese general merchandise (green tea, black tea, Japanese orange, silk piece goods, lacquer ware, camphor, matting and so on), the wheat crop yield of Prairie regions, tariffs and regulations of exports and imports and so on. These pieces of information were sent from Japanese consuls of New York, Chicago, Sydney, Lyon, Hong Kong, Vancouver, Montreal and Vancouver.

3. Canada as a Market of Japanese Green Tea

Figure 1 shows the general trend regarding Japan's trade with Canada between the late nineteenth century and the early twentieth century based on the *Statistical Yearbook of Japanese Empire* published every year since 1882 by Japan's Cabinet Statistical Bureau. Japanese exports to Canada consistently exceeded her imports. This trend generally continued until 1922-23, when Canada's exports to Japan exceeded its imports for the first time.

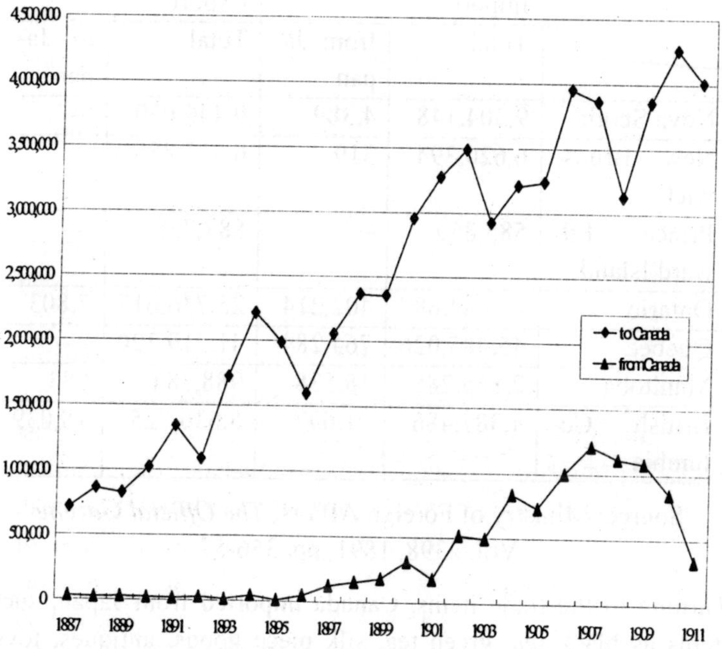

Figure 1 Japan's Trade with Canada, 1887-1911 (Japanese yen)
Source: *Statistical Yearbook of Japanese Empire*, each year.

The majority of Japanese exports to Canada directed to the two central provinces of Ontario and Quebec. In 1890, 31.96 per cent of Japan's total exports to Canada went to Ontario, and 60.73 per cent of that went to Quebec. It must be noted that although the British Columbia imports occupied only 5.70 per cent of all Canadian imports from Japan in the same year, British Columbia's trade structure, compared with the rest of Canada, was characterized by more reliance upon Japan than any other province. See Table 2.

Table 2 Japanese Trade with Canada by provinces 1890 (dollar)

	Import		Export	
	Total	from Japan	Total	to Japan
Nova Scotia	9,304,148	4,389	9,440,639	—
New Brunswick	6,620,394	319	6,977,855	—
Prince Edward Island	585,859	—	887,755	—
Ontario	43,684,687	402,214	25,736,617	7,803
Quebec	45,485,026	764,284	41,719,320	—
Manitoba	2,555,285	15,538	988,384	983
British Columbia	4,387,486	71,697	5,636,725	18,039

Source: Ministry of Foreign Affairs, *The Official Gazette* Vol. 2398, 1891, pp. 356-57

Turning to the trade items, Canada imported from Japan, such items as black tea, green tea, silk piece goods, antiques, toys, cotton textiles, and pottery and so on. Among these trading items, green tea consistently hosted more than 80 per cent of the total exports to Canada in the late nineteenth century. The following two items, rice and silk, comprised 3-10 per cent of the total exports to Canada in the same period. On the other hand, Canadian exports to Japan were mainly lumber, coal and flour; lumber accounted for about 30 per cent in the late 1880s, but came to account for about 50 per cent in the 1890s.

Although small in relative terms, trade with Canada was of increasing importance from the late nineteenth century. In particular exports of tea, rice and silk, and imports of lumber and flour were all becoming important as Japan became industrial-ized. Among these trading items, tea trade was a key factor regarding Japan's trade with Canada.

Japan's leading exports were tea and raw silk during the period of 1860-1895, but Japan's traditional tea was green, not black. This was very interesting and important thing to research the Japanese economic development from the end of Tokugawa era (Tsunoyama, 1980). According to *the British Consular Reports on the Production of Tea in Japan* published in 1873,

> Japan teas find very little sale in the English market. . . . Most of it finds its way to the United States or Canada. . . . The taste for teas differs in America and in England. In America the prevailing taste is for green or uncoloured teas, while in England it is for black teas, and it has been found easier and more profitable to prepare Japan teas as the former than as the latter.

From this report, it can be seen that Japan's tea trade was almost exclusively dependent upon the North American markets.

In 1873, Canadian merchants imported $1,496,785 of green tea from China, while imported merely of $166,605 from Japan. A decade later, Canada's green tea imports from Japan became nearly equivalent to the one from China, and Japan completely surpassed China as a Canadian source of tea supply in another decade. I do not know the reason why Japan supplanted China as Canada's first important tea trading partner, but it is certain that Japanese tea was preferred to Chinese tea for Canadian people.

In spite of the smaller markets, the Meiji Government considered Canada as a prospective market in this period, not only because Canada was potentially huge market, but also because the Canadian consumed tea much more than the American people did. According to the Consular Report of 15 August 1897 (*The Journal of Commercial Reports* Vol. 78), the average tea consumption of Canada from 1873 to 1895 had been as follows; 2.85 pound in 1868 to 1872, 3.84 pound in 1873 to 1877, 3.41 pound in 1878 to 1882, 4.12 pound in 1883 to 1887, 3.91 pound in 1888 to 1892, 3.95 pound in 1893, 4.07 pound in 1894, 4.08

pound in 1895. The annual consumption per capita in the U.S. was merely 1.38 pound on an average in 1897.

Turning to the distribution of tea, black tea was evenly divided among all regions, on the other hand, green tea was imported by two regions, Ontario and Quebec. Table 3 and Table 4 show the volume of tea trade by regions in Canada from 1888 to 1896.

Table 3 Imports of Black Tea to Canada by Regions 1888-1896

	1888		1890		1892		1894		1896	
	price	pound	price	pound	price	pound	price	pound	price	pound
N.S.	321	1,784	390	2,539	312	1,891	328	2,230	338	2,146
N.B.	269	1,510	262	552	215	1,286	261	1,740	346	1,547
P.E.I.	103	549	71	423	64	370	75	449	57	332
Ontario	299	1,467	420	2,234	449	2,375	391	2,382	566	3,671
Quebec	254	1,447	335	1,899	305	1,819	357	2,336	310	2,127
Manitoba	78	435	59	366	85	396	93	652	138	954
B.C.	60	267	46	256	119	803	80	533	74	581
N.T.	—	—	—	—	—	—	—	—	0.36	2.56

Price: 1,000 dollars, pound: 1,000 pounds

Source: *The Journal of Commercial Reports*, Vol. 78, 1897, pp. 18-21

Table 4 Imports of Green Tea to Canada by Regions 1888-1896

	1888		1890		1892		1894		1896	
	price	pound	price	pound	price	pound	price	pound	price	pound
N. S.	—	—	0.51	2.8	0.3	1.2	—	—	—	—
Ontario	717	4,371	587	3,676	852	5,477	79	5,587	88	6,824
Quebec	893	5,243	828	5,413	1,206	7,953	653	4,497	615	4,743
Manitoba	12	80	80	6.7	47	179	12	92	10	103
B. C.	45	242	37	241	22	161	7	47	4	33

Price: 1,000 dollars, pound: 1,000 pounds

Source: *The Journal of Commercial Reports*, Vol. 78, 1897, pp. 18-21

In the case of black tea, Ontario, Quebec, Nova Scotia, and New Brunswick, these four made up around 20 per cent respectively in this period. On the other hand, in case of green tea, Ontario and Quebec was overwhelming, accounted for over 90 per cent. But Quebec share rose sharply from 1894, and came to account for about 85 per cent. It is clear that the majority of Japanese green tea exports to Canada went direct to central Canada. Thus, the Japanese Government needed to set up a consulate in central

Canada as well as the Pacific coast in order to maintain demand for Japanese green tea, and to enjoy a robust and vibrant economic relationship with Canada.

4. Concluding Remarks

As mentioned above, it was very profitable for Japan to trade with Canada during the late nineteenth century. Despite the prospect of steady expansion, however, demand for Japanese goods, except for tea, grew more slowly than had been anticipated.

The opening of the Pacific Ocean regular route between Vancouver and Yokohama in 1887 and the establishment of Japanese Consulate in Vancouver in 1889 were expected to facilitate Japanese-Canadian trade, but large-scale trade did not begin until the 1900s. This slow start frustrated government offices as well as Japanese merchants. According to the Japanese consular report (*Journal of Commercial Reports*, vol. 81, 1897, pp. 50-52), there were two serious problems to overcome in order to expand the Japanese trade relationship with Canada.

(1) The first problem was that in manufacturing, Japanese manufactured goods; especially umbrellas, silk textile, china and pottery ware, faced severe competition with German manufacture.

(2) The second problem was that Japanese merchants had to penetrate into existing Western merchant networks.

These difficulties discouraged the Japanese merchants and business persons from trading with Canada.

Fukashi Sugimura, the first consul in Canada, had recognized the Pacific region and the Atlantic region as two distinct markets, but it seemed that he had not recognized the U.S. and Canada as two different markets after his undertaking investigation on the Canadian economic conditions in his first year. He pointed out in his report dated 14 November 1889, in order to encourage the development of trade with Canada and the trade to be carried out through the Japanese merchants themselves, I shall recommend that general company, such as Mitsui, will establish the branch office in Canada and directly receive orders from Canadian traders.

However, in the consular report from Vancouver in 1897 we find only one Japanese merchant staying in central Canada. His name was Ishikawa-Shoten. According to the consular report, he was active in importing tea, Japanese rice, silk cloth and so on. In addition there were only three reliable agents in Montreal engaged in importing Japanese goods mainly from Yokohama. Under these circumstances, it was not until 1901 that the Japanese government set up the consulate in Montreal—two years later, moved to Ottawa—in order to respond to the new market situation. As a result of this, relevant information was finally passed on to small and middle-sized industrialists, traders and farmers, turning a new page in the early Japanese—Canadian commercial relations history.

References

Kitagawa, Katsuhiko, 1997, *A Study of Japan's Economic Relations with South Africa*, Nichibunken-Sosho (in Japanese).

Sugihara, Kaoru, 1996, *The Emergence and Structure of intra-Asian Trade*, Minerva (in Japanese).

Tsunoyama, Sakae, 1980, *A Study of Tea History*, Chu-Kou Shinsho (in Japanese).

_____, ed. 1986, *A Study of Japanese Consular Reports*, Dobunkan (in Japanese).

Ecological Footprint in Canada and Israel—Toward Innovative Policy Tool

DAN GOTTLIEB
School of Political Science
University of Haifa, Israel

Section 1: The Ecological Footprint—A Canadian Innovative Concept for Sustainability

The morning alarm rings. You take a hot shower, brew up a cup of coffee, read a bit from the morning newspaper and hop in the car to get to work on time. Have you ever stopped to consider the total environmental impact involved in each of these daily habits? Or, simply asked yourself: "Just how much of the Earth is dedicated to sustaining just me?" Not many of us have done so—we simply do not think of ourselves as ecological entities. Urbanization, trade, technology, globalization and no less important, life-style choices have alienated modern human beings from ecological systems.

The question I began with: "Just how much of the Earth is dedicated to sustaining ourselves?" is becoming one of the most important and urgent questions in our time. In the debate over environmental problems, more and more pressure is gradually being focused upon the individual choices that we make in everyday life. At the United Nations Conference on Environment and Development which took place in Rio de Janeiro in 1992, a comprehensive blueprint, called Agenda 21, was created and outlined, which stated that over-consumption must be halted if we are to live sustainability. The term sustainability means "meeting the needs of the present without compromising the ability of future generations to meet their own needs." (World Commission on Environment and Development, 1987)

Regarding this question, two scientists from the University of British Columbia in Canada, Prof. William Rees and his former student, Dr. Mathis Wackerangel, developed during the 1990s an indicator that they called the Ecological Footprint. The starting point of Rees and Wackerangel was that even if you are a hi-tech employee who lives in a penthouse in Vancouver, Tel-Aviv or Sydney, and does his shopping via the Internet without leaving home, you still do not live a virtual life. In other words, you have an impact on the natural environment and that impact can be measured.

By definition, Ecological Footprint analysis is an accounting tool that enables us to estimate the resource consumption and waste assimilation requirements of a defined human population in terms of a corresponding productive land area. In other words, the ecological footprint aims to represent demands put on the environment by human activities in term of consumed land all over the globe.

The ecological footprint starts from the assumption that every category of energy and material consumption and waste discharge requires the productive or absorptive capacity of a finite area of land or water. If we sum up the land requirements for all categories of consumption and waste discharge by a defined population, the total area wherever it may be, represents the ecological footprint of that population.

When undertaking an ecological Footprint analysis, as developed by Rees & Wackerangel (1996), it is convenient to distinguish between the following categories of land as expressed in the graphics:

> The first category (from left to right) is 'energy land' expressed by the area somewhere on earth that is needed to absorb our emissions of carbon dioxide produced by energy consumption.
>
> The second category is consumed land or 'built land' that is occupied by human settlements and infrastructures.

The third category is 'farm land' which is the area required to grow food and fiber. This in turn is subdivided into various land types such as: arable land, which is biologically speaking the most productive land, and pasture land, which is used primarily for grazing cattle.

The fourth category is forest land which refers to forests that can yield timber products.

Ecological Footprint results are expressed in single measurement unit called Global Hectares (GH). A global hectare is a measure of land that is estimated to have the world average productivity of all biologically productive land. Because of international trade and the dispersion of waste and pollution, the hectares in demand can be physically located anywhere in the world.

Let us illustrate the ecological footprint concept by a simple activity—driving a car.

What are the total land areas that we need to sustain this activity?

- First and foremost, the car requires built-up land to drive upon.
- Energy land—the associated land area needed to sequester the CO2 emissions of the car.

By adding the estimates for built land to energy land we get the car travel footprint, which is a part of the total ecological footprint of a person, a community, a nation or humanity as a whole.

If the ecological footprint represents human demand upon nature, it should be compared with Nature's supply, or in other words—bio-capacity. Bio-capacity has been defined by Kiznetz et al. (2007) as the capacity of ecosystems to produce useful biological materials and to absorb waste materials generated by humans. Like the ecological footprint, bio-capacity is usually calculated for all biologically productive land and sea areas on the planet and is expressed by Global Hectares.

It is beyond the scope of this lecture to discuss in detail about the methodology used in calculating the ecological footprint. Nevertheless, it is important to say that based on data from

2003, the amount of bio-capacity available on the planet per person is 1.8 GH. During the same year, human demand upon nature e.g. the total ecological footprint of humanity in per capita terms was 2.2 GH. This situation in which the ecological footprint exceeds available bio-capacity is known as overshoot. Beyond a certain point, the material growth of the world economy can be purchased only at the expense of depleting natural capital and undermining the life support services upon which we all depend.

Section 2: Ecological Footprint of Canada and Israel—National Perspectives

On national scale, the average Canadian ecological footprint is about 7.6 GH per person. This is about four times greater than the amount of bio-capacity that the Earth can provide for each person (1.8 GH), which means it takes 7.6 hectares of land and sea throughout the world to support each Canadian. The good news is that Canadians are fortunate in having a surplus of natural capital. Canada's available bio-capacity is significant with 14.5 GH per capita.

For the time being, Canada's bio-capacity remains larger than its oversized ecological footprint, mostly due to a vast forest area. However, this does not mean that Canada's natural environment can support more consumption. As Canada's population increases, its bio-capacity will have to be shared among more people—which means that the per capita of bio-capacity is shrinking. Furthermore, even if Canadians enjoy a domestic surplus of natural capital, from a global viewpoint Canadian citizens as other nations have to confine themselves to their fair share per capita which is 1.8 GH.

Canada is one of the few countries with a high rate of available bio-capacity per capita (14.5 GH) and therefore is a leader state in terms of providing ecological services and products to the globe. These services and products include its absorption of CO_2 by forest land, its timber products, and being one of the most important wheat suppliers in the world. Canada, from a bio-capacity perspective, has an important role in stabilizing social and political systems against a background of turmoil as a result of rising prices and a shortage of food products, especially among developing nations.

If we look at the ecological footprint of Israel, we see that the average person has a 4.6 GH ecological footprint. This is more than twice the amount of bio-capacity that the earth can provide for each person. Compared to Canada, Israelis have only 0.4 GH per capita of bio-capacity. Such a low bio-capacity rate in Israel can be explained by accelerated urbanization, high natural birth rate and immigration. Like Canada, Israel has still a long way to go to confine itself to its fair share per capita (Global Footprint Network, 2006).

Section 3: The Ecological Footprint as Policy Tool

The ecological footprint analysis enables policy-makers and planners to explore different scenarios of development and adopt the less harmful scenario in terms of ecological footprint, especially in the fields of energy use and land-use management. Furthermore, the ecological footprint's information divided to its components is a required input for setting prioritized goals for the implementation of policies aimed at reducing the ecological footprint of the city and the nation. In this sense, the ecological footprint makes the sustainability challenge more transparent, and decision makers have an ecological criterion for ranking policy, project or technological options. So far, studies dealing with the 'Ecological Footprint' have focused on the estimated size of the ecological footprint in the local and national scale, on the relative sizes of its components, and on developing the calculation methodology. It has not yet explored the significance of the ecological footprint as a policy tool. I believe that from this perspective, the ecological footprint offers a new agenda of research for the social sciences, and especially for policy and planning studies and practice.

Summary

The ecological footprint developed in Canada is not just an index or calculation tool but is a reality that was hidden behind the curtain of economic growth and globalization. In that context, we are the first generation that has the tools to remove this curtain, understand the impact of human activity on the natural environment, and not less important to change our way of life in order to achieve not just environmental sustainability but also social and economic stability for us and for future generations.

References

Wackerangel, M. & W. Rees. 1996. Our Ecological Footprint: Reducing human impact on earth. USA: New Society publication.

Global Footprint Network. 2006. National footprint accounts—datasheets.

Energy Cooperation between Canada and South Korea: Canadian Oil Sands

SE HYUN AHN
University of Seoul, Korea

Energy Potentials of Canada

Canada has considerable natural resources and is one of the world's largest producers and exporters of energy. Canada was the fifth-largest energy producer in the world in 2000, behind the United States, Russia, China, and Saudi Arabia. Over the past two decades, Canada has become a significant net energy exporter. Canada is a net exporter of oil, natural gas, coal, uranium, and hydropower.

In 2005, Canada produced 19.1 quadrillion British Thermal Units (Btu) of total energy, the fifth-largest amount in the world. Since 1980, Canada's total energy production has increased by 86 percent, while its total energy consumption has increased by only 48 percent during that period.

It is also one of the most important sources of US energy imports. Almost all of Canada's energy exports go to the United States, making it the largest foreign source of U.S. energy imports: Canada is consistently among the top sources for U.S. oil imports, and it is the largest source of U.S. natural gas and electricity imports. Recognizing the importance of the energy trade between the two countries, both participate in the North American Energy Working Group, which seeks to improve energy integration and cooperation between Canada, the U.S., and Mexico.[1] In 2000, for example, about 30% of Canadian energy production was exported, with the United States by far its main customer. From January through August 2002, the United States imported more oil (including crude oil and petroleum products) from Canada than from any other country. The United States also imported about 2.2 tcf of Canadian natural gas in the first seven months of 2002, with 93% of total US gas imports coming from Canada.[2]

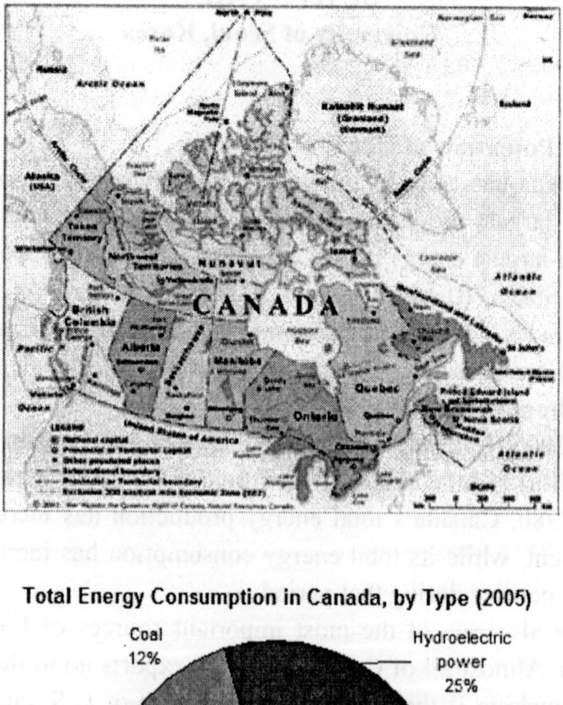

Total Energy Consumption in Canada, by Type (2005)

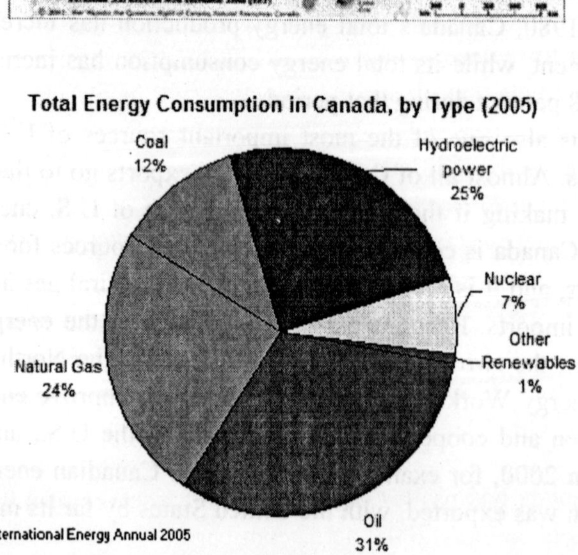

Source: International Energy Annual 2005

In 2005, as the above figure indicates, the largest source of energy consumption in Canada was oil (31 percent), followed by hydroelectricity (25 percent) and natural gas (24 percent). Both coal (12 percent) and nuclear (7 percent) constitute a smaller share of the country's overall energy mix. From 1985-2005, Canada's overall energy mix has remained relatively stable, though hydroelectricity has decreased from 31 percent to 25 percent.

In 2000, about 36% of Canada's primary energy production was natural gas, followed by oil (23%), hydropower (20%), coal (11%), and nuclear power (4%). Over two-thirds of Canada's energy is produced in the province of Alberta.

Besides being a major producer, Canada is also a significant energy consumer and a member of the International Energy Agency (IEA). Canada was the world's fifth-largest energy consumer in 2000, roughly on par with India in terms of total energy consumption. Canada has the highest energy intensity of any OECD country.

Canada's total oil production (including all liquids) was 3.36 million bbl/d in 2007. The country's oil production has steadily increased as new oil sands and offshore projects have come on-stream to replace aging fields in the western province. Overall, EIA predicts that oil sands production will increase even further in coming years and more than offset the decline in Canada's conventional crude oil production: according to the May 2008 *Short Term Energy Outlook*, EIA expects Canadian oil production to increase to 3.42 million bbl/d in 2008 and 3.59 million bbl/d in 2009. Canada consumed an estimated 2.34 million bbl/d of oil in 2007. The country sends over 99 percent of its oil exports to the U.S., and it is consistently one of the top three sources of U.S. oil imports.[3]

Oil

Canada has proven conventional oil reserves of 4.9 bn barrels, as of January 2002, a 152-mm-barrel increase over January

2001 reserves. Oil production averaged 2.9 mm bpd during 2002, with estimated consumption of 2.0 mm bpd. The province of Alberta, located in western Canada, is by far the country's leading oil producing region.

While Alberta's light oil reserves are declining (the province now contains an estimated 45% of the country's total light oil reserves), the province also contains huge oil sands deposits. Meanwhile, projects and potential projects in other provinces are shifting the oil industry's focus to include the eastern and northern parts of the country.

Canada is a major source of US oil imports. From January through August 2002, the United States imported 1.89 mm bpd of oil from Canada (1.39 mm bpd of which was crude oil). This makes Canada the top petroleum supplier to the United States and the third-largest supplier of crude oil imports (behind Saudi Arabia and Mexico, and ahead of Venezuela). Canada has been the top supplier to the United States of refined petroleum products, including gasoline, jet fuel, distillate, etc., over the past few years.

Oil Sector Organization & Trends

Canada has a privatized oil sector that has witnessed consolidation in recent years. The largest integrated operator in the country is Imperial Oil, majority owned by ExxonMobil. Canada's oil sector has seen also significant mergers and acquisitions in recent years, with US firms purchasing over $ 35 bn in Canadian oil and gas assets during 2001. In July 2001, Houston-based Conoco purchased Gulf Canada for $ 8.9 bn, marking the largest oil and gas deal in Canadian history. In October 2001, Devon Energy (US) acquired Canada's Anderson Exploration for $ 7.1 bn. In December, 2001, Burlington Resources (US) purchased Canada's Canadian Hunter Resources for $ 3.4 bn. In addition, Canadian firms also have been busy reorganizing the country's oil patch. In April 2002, two of Canada's largest companies, Alberta Energy and PanCanadian, also merged to create

EnCana, the world's largest independent oil and natural gas producer (by market value). Other significant oil producers in Canada include Exxon's Imperial Oil, Shell's Shell Canada, Petro-Canada, Talisman Energy, Suncor, EOG Resources, Husky Energy, and Apache Canada.[4]

Canada's oil sands producers have also attracted increasing attention from Asian oil companies, seeking to satisfy growing demand in their countries and secure equity oil stakes. In July 2006, state-run Korea National Oil Corporation (KNOC) purchased the BlackGold bitumen deposit from Newmont for $250 million; BlackGold contains an estimated 250 million barrels of crude oil, and KNOC plans to bring 35,000 bbl/d of production onstream at the site by 2010.

China's Sinopec earlier purchased a 40 percent stake in the Syneco's Northern Lights oil sands project, which Syneco plans to bring online in 2010 at a production rate of 100,000 bbl/d. In addition, the China National Offshore Oil Corporation (CNOOC) holds a stake in MEG Energy, a subsidiary of EnCana that operates the Christina Lake project. In 2007, the Chinese National Petroleum company (CNPC) won exploration rights for a 260-acre tract in Alberta.[5]

Top Western Hemisphere Oil Producers, 2007

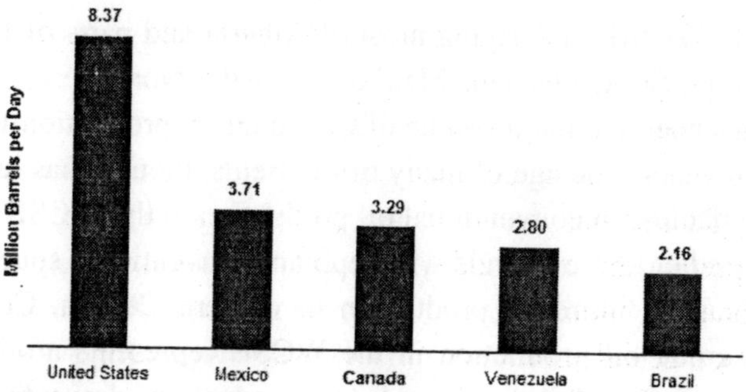

Source: EIA International Petroleum Monthly

Exploration and Production

Western Canada, and more specifically Alberta, remains the premier energy producing region in Canada. The Western Canadian Sedimentary Basin, underlying Alberta, Saskatchewan, and part of the Northwest Territories, has been the main source of Canadian oil production for the past 50 years. An estimated 60% of conventional oil production in 2000 came from Alberta.

However, conventional oil production has been declining in the West as it has been rising in the East in the last few years. Exploration and production activity on Canada's east coast is focused on the Jeanne d'Arc Basin, offshore Newfoundland. The climate demands technologically advanced offshore oil platforms, able to withstand extremely cold temperatures and high winds, which add to production costs.

Canadian oil production comes mainly from three sources: the Western Canada Sedimentary Basin (WCSB); the oil sands deposits of northern Alberta; and offshore fields in the Atlantic Ocean. Alberta contains the largest share of Canada's oil production, as it holds the majority of oil sands deposits and the bulk of the WCSB. According to Statistics Canada, Alberta represented 68 percent of Canada's national oil production in 2007.[6]

Western Canada Sedimentary Basin

The WCSB, underlying most of Alberta and parts of British Columbia, Saskatchewan, Manitoba and the Northwest Territories, has been the main source of Canadian oil production for the past 50 years. The age of many of the fields, though, has led to a steady decline in conventional oil production in the WCSB. Analysts predict that oil sands will supplant conventional sources as the focus of future oil production in western Canada. Conventional crude oil production in the WCSB represents around 38 percent of Canada's total crude oil production, down from 65 percent in 1999.

Offshore

Canada has three oil projects off its Atlantic coastline, all located in the Jeanne d'Arc Basin: Hibernia (135,000 bbl/d, Petro-Canada), Terra Nova (116,000 bbl/d, Petro-Canada), and White Rose (117,000 bbl/d, Husky). The basin has seen an increase in investment plans in recent years, with both White Rose and Hibernia announcing plans to expand production by incorporating satellite fields. Outside of the Jeanne d'Arc Basin, StatoilHydro announced in 2008 that it would begin a drilling program at the Mizzen field in the Flemish Pass basin. Chevron signed a MOU with the provincial government in 2007 to develop the Hebron-Ben Nevis field, which could hold recoverable reserves of 700 million barrels. Operators at the Atlantic oil fields must contend with harsh natural conditions, including rough seas, seasonal icebergs, and extreme temperatures. These factors increase the difficulty and costs of oil production in the region.

Off the Pacific coast, industry experts believe that there could be sizable oil and natural gas reserves. However, there has been no production to date there, because of a federal ban on offshore oil activities in the Pacific Ocean.[7]

Pipelines

Although most Canadian oil is produced in western Canada (mainly Alberta), oil is consumed primarily in central and eastern Canada. As a result, Canada exports mostly crude oil from Alberta and imports crude oil and petroleum products on the east coast, explaining why Canada exports approximately 1.89 mm bpd (gross) to the United States, but net exports are slightly lower (1.78 mm bpd).

Domestic System

An extensive pipeline system transports western Canadian oil to domestic and U.S. markets. There are two major oil pipeline operators in Canada: Enbridge Pipelines and Kinder Morgan Canada (formerly Terasen). Enbridge operates a 9,000-mile network of pipelines and terminals, delivering oil from Edmonton, Alberta, to eastern Canada and the U.S. Great Lakes region. Kinder Morgan operates the Trans Mountain Pipe Line (TMPL), which delivers oil mainly from Alberta west to refineries and terminals in the Vancouver, British Columbia area. The expansion of Alberta's oil sands industry has necessitated the construction of several new pipelines to transport diluted bitumen and synthetic crude to downstream facilities in the Edmonton area.

Export Pipelines

Canada has extensive oil pipeline connections with the United States. Enbridge maintains connections between major Canadian cities and Chicago, integrating the Canadian and U.S. components of its network. Enbridge also operates Spearhead, a 650-mile pipeline with a capacity of 125,000-bbl/d that links Chicago with Cushing, Oklahoma; originally carrying oil from Cushing to Chicago, Enbridge received regulatory approval in late 2004 to reverse the flow of the pipeline, allowing it to export oil from Canada deeper into the U.S. market.

Kinder Morgan exports oil to the U.S. through an extension of the TMPL that reaches northern Washington. It also operates Express, a 790-mile, 170,000-bbl/d pipeline that links Hardisty, Alberta and Casper, Wyoming; from Casper, the company's 930-mile, 120,000-bbl/d Platte pipeline runs to Wood River, Illinois.

Any increase in oil sands production will require additional pipeline capacity to take that production to world markets. Along with expanding existing trunk lines, Enbridge has proposed a new pipeline linking the Chicago area with the U.S. Gulf Coast, which would allow oil sands producers greater access to the large concentration of refineries there. Enbridge has floated plans for the construction of the 720-mile, 400,000-bbl/d Gateway pipeline from Edmonton to Kitimat, a deepwater port in British Columbia capable of supporting very large crude carriers (VLCC). The Gateway pipeline would facilitate the export of oil sands to Asia and California. Kinder Morgan has discussed plans to build a similar pipeline or upgrade the capacity of the TMPL.

Import Pipelines

Enbridge has proposed construction of the Southern Lights pipeline, which would transport 180,000 bbl/d of light hydrocarbons from Chicago to Edmonton. Oil sands operators in Alberta rely on these hydrocarbons to dilute bitumen so that it can flow through pipelines. Currently, the largest source of diluents comes from natural gas liquids, however the prospects of declining Canadian natural gas production mean that Alberta could face a diluents crunch without additional supplies.

Oil Exports and Imports

In 2007, Canada exported 2.4 million bbl/d of crude oil and refined products to the U.S., the single-largest source of U.S. oil imports. The largest share of U.S.-bound Canadian oil exports go to the Midwest (PAD District II), followed by the Rocky Mountains (PAD District IV). The bulk of Canadian exports to the U.S. have traditionally gone to PAD Districts II, because this area is well connected to Alberta by oil pipelines and not well served by coastal import terminals in the U.S.[8]

Canadian Oil Sands

Second only to the Saudi Arabia reserves, Alberta's oil sands deposits are described as "Canada's greatest buried energy treasure," and could satisfy the world's demand for petroleum for the next century. They are contained in three major areas beneath 140,200* square kilometres of north-eastern Alberta—an area larger than the state of Florida, an area twice the size of New Brunswick, more than four and half times the size of Vancouver Island, and 26 times larger than Prince Edward Island. However, only about two per cent of the initial established resource has been produced to date.

Oil sands contain deposits of bitumen, a heavy, viscous oil. There are two methods currently used to extract bitumen from the ground: open pit mining and *in situ* ("in place"). Open pit mining resembles conventional mining techniques and is effective in extracting oil sands deposits near the surface. However, the bulk of Canada's estimated oil sands deposits (80 percent) are too deep below the surface to use open pit mining. The second method, *in situ*,can reach these deeper deposits. *In situ* extraction involves the use of steam to separate bitumen from the surrounding sands and lift it to collection pools near the surface. To date, Canadian oil sands producers have employed each method almost equally, but future production will likely shift to emphasize *in situ* extraction. Once extracted, oil sands producers must add lighter hydrocarbons to the bitumen to allow it to flow through pipelines. Upgraders then process most of the bitumen into "synthetic crude," which can then be sold to a traditional oil refinery, though some bitumen is also sold in raw form for the production of heavy products like tar and asphalt. Some oil sands projects have integrated upgrading capacity, while others must send their raw bitumen production to another facility.

In 2007, oil sands production represented approximately half of Canada's total crude oil production. The Athabasca oil sands deposit in northern Alberta is one of largest oil sands deposits in the world. There are also sizable oil sands deposits on Melville Island in the Canadian Arctic, and two smaller deposits in northern Alberta near Cold Lake and Peace River.

The largest oil sands projects in the Athabasca area utilize open-pit mining. The Syncrude Project, operated by Canadian Oil Sands Limited, produced 258,000 bbl/d of synthetic crude in 2006. Suncor operates another large open-pit mining project in Alberta, which produced 236,000 bbl/d of crude oil in 2007. Finally, the Athabasca Oil Sands Project (AOSP), operated by Shell Canada, began production in 2002 and currently has a capacity of 155,000 bbl/d. AOSP utilizes a facility adjacent to

Shell's Scotford refinery to upgrade raw bitumen produced by the project.

The *in situ* oil sands projects in the Athabasca area are smaller than their mining counterparts. In 2004, Suncor began operations at its Firebag project, which utilizes a relatively new *in situ* technology called steam-assisted gravity drainage (SAGD). Other SAGD projects include Petro-Canada's MacKay River and Dover; EnCana's Foster Creek and Christina Lake; and Nexen's Athabasca and Long Lake. Petro-Canada's Dover facility also contains a demonstration project of a new *in situ* technology called vapour extraction (VAPEX). VAPEX utilizes solvents, such as butane, to extract raw bitumen, rather than steam; VAPEX could allow significant cost savings for *in situ* operators, since the operators can re-use most of the solvents.

Outside of the Athabasca deposit, the largest oil sands project is Imperial Oil's Cold Lake *in situ* facility, with a capacity of 150,000 bbl/d. Also in the Cold Lake area, CNRL operates Primrose, while Husky operates the Tucker project. In the Peace River deposit, Shell Canada operates Cadotte Lake (11,000 bbl/d).

Despite the excitement surrounding the development of Canada's oil sands reserves, there are still several difficulties that could impede the future development of the industry. Analysts predict that the production of synthetic crude from oil sands is only economically viable with relatively high crude oil prices. While further advances in oil sands technology could reduce production costs, it is likely that synthetic oil production will continue to be dependent upon high crude oil prices.

Second, the oil sands industry is heavily reliant upon water and natural gas, which is necessary in both the extraction of bitumen from oil sands and the upgrading of bitumen to synthetic oil. Even though there have been some efforts to reduce this dependence on natural gas, any increase in natural gas prices or sharp reduction in natural gas supply would have critical repercussions for the oil sands industry. Newer technologies could reduce the need for natural gas, such as the aforementioned VAPEX *in situ* process. Another technique in development is called toe-to-heel air inhection (THAI), where bitumen is ignited in the ground to warm the reserves, then pumped with horizontal wells. Finally, there has been some discussion of the potential of using nuclear power plants to provide energy for steam generation, though no one has developed any concrete plans to implement this approach. In any event, water or natural gas constraints in the area put downward pressure on any forecast of future oil sands production (see below).

Finally, there are reports that the oil sands boom is creating a labour shortage in Alberta's oil industry, especially in Fort McMurray. This has led to an escalation in labour costs and construction delays due to a lack of available workers. Several companies planning or developing oil sands projects have significantly increased their cost estimates due to rising prices for labour, materials, and support services. In 2005, Shell Canada announced that the planned costs for its proposed 100,000-bbl/d expansion of the AOSP project had increased from C$4 billion to C$7 billion; in 2006, Western Oil Sands, a stakeholder in the AOSP project, warned that these costs could rise even further to C$11 billion. Along with labour issues, oil sands projects must also face the challenges of the generally tight global market for industrial goods and engineering services.

Even considering these concerns, most forecasts of world oil markets estimate that Canadian oil sands will become an increasingly important component of world oil supply. EIA's *International Energy Outlook 2006* (IEO) estimates that Canadian oil sands operators will produce 3.6 million bbl/d by 2030.

In fact, much of the exploration in Alberta in coming years likely will be for heavy crude and oil sands, as conventional oil reserves are being depleted. Unlike conventional oil, oil sands contain a mixture of bitumen, sand, water and clay. Bitumen, which is a thick and tar-like hydrocarbon, surrounds the sand and water.

To develop oil sands, bitumen is separated from the sand, water and clay. Once separated, bitumen can be upgraded into a high-quality oil called "synthetic crude." One of the largest synthetic crude producers, Syncrude (a joint venture of Alberta Energy, Canadian Oil Sands Investments, Conoco, Imperial, Mocal Energy, Murphy Oil, Nexen, and Petro-Canada), reported an average production cost of about $ 11.50 per barrel in 2001.

Canada holds between 1.7 and 2.5 tons barrels of oil sands. The Athabasca Oil Sands deposit, in northern Alberta, is one of the two largest oil sands deposits in the world (the other is in the Orinoco Belt, Venezuela). There are also oil sands deposits on Melville Island, in the Canadian Arctic, and there are three smaller deposits in northern Alberta.

Current output of synthetic crude and bitumen is estimated at 600,000 bpd. A new oil sands project, the Muskeg River Mine, located on the Athabasca oil sands and operated by Shell Canada, Western Oil Sands and Chevron Canada, is scheduled to begin production in early 2003. The Muskeg River mine will produce an additional 155,000 bpd. Construction also is nearing completion at Petro-Canada's MacKay River oil sands project. Petro-Canada expects production of 30,000 bpd in 2003. According to the Canadian government, synthetic oil and bitumen production is expected to reach 1.2 mm bpd by 2010.

There have been four epochs of development of Canada's oil sands.

Exploration Phase: 1700 to 1919

Scientific Phase: 1920 to 1929

Testing Phase: 1930 to 1959

Commercialization Phase: 1960 to 1997[9]

Alberta Energy appears to be quite attractive because of the responsible development of these extensive deposits through planning and liaison with government, industry and communities to ensure a competitive royalty regime that is attractive to investors, appropriate regulations and environmental protection and the management of Crown rights to oil sands while taking into account some of the barriers—higher technological risk and higher capital costs—faced by oil sands developers.

Alberta's oil sands industry was possible due to multi-billion-dollar investments in infrastructure and technology required to develop the non-conventional resource. According to the Canadian Association of Petroleum Producers (CAPP), in 2006 industry investment in Alberta's oil sands reached approximately $14 billion.

In 2006, Alberta's oil sands were the source of about 62 per cent of the province's total crude oil and equivalent production and about 47 per cent of all crude oil and equivalent produced in Canada. Over the last four fiscal years, from 2003/2004 to 2006/2007, oil sands development returned $4.276 billion to Albertans in the form of royalties paid to the provincial government.[10]

Annual oil sands production is growing steadily as the industry matures. Output of marketable oil sands production increased to 1.126 million barrels per day (bbl/d) in 2006. With anticipated growth, this level of production could reach 3 million barrels per day by 2020 and possibly even 5 million barrels per day by 2030. This degree of activity would support the development of other key industries and see Alberta become a Global Energy Leader.[11]

Development of Alberta's oil sands resources represents a triumph of technological innovation. Over the years, government and industry have worked together to find innovative and economic ways to extract and process the oil sands and energy research is more important today than ever before. Working through the Alberta Energy Research Institute, the Alberta government is committed to a collaborative approach to spur new technology and innovation programs that will reduce the impact of greenhouse gases and other emissions, and reduce the consumption of water and gas.

Important Factors for Oil Sands

Crude Oil Prices

By far the most important factor in the profitability equation is the price of the conventional crude oil. Low prices have historically indicated excess supply, low demand or both and made it extremely difficult for oil sands producers to breakeven. However, the high price environment up to the middle of 2008 is excellent for the development of Canada's oil sands and their profitability. The uptrend is a result of growing global demand, depletion of existing reserves and a lack of growth in new oil supplies.[12]

Natural Gas Prices

Natural gas use is a major cost for oil sands producers. Natural gas is used to heat up the water that is used to separate the bitumen from the oil sands in mining projects. It is also used in the upgrading process to convert the bitumen to synthetic crude oil. For in situ projects, natural gas is used to create steam that is directly injected in the reservoir to lower the viscosity of the bitumen. In short the cost of natural gas is one of the largest variable costs. Companies that can use natural gas more efficiently or can eliminate the use of natural gas in the production of Canada's oil sands will have a significant cost advantage in the future. Natural gas is the largest operating expense for in situ oil sands projects, representing 60% of all operating costs. Mining operations use far less natural gas but it still represents 15% of total operating costs.[13]

South Korea's Involvement in Alberta's Oil Sands

South Korea has been hunting for investment opportunities in Alberta's oil sands to improve its security of supply since 2000. The Alberta government had assisted KNOC since 2000 to explore investment options in the oil sands, where recoverable reserves are estimated at 300 bn barrels. From the beginning

KNOC had no interest in owning shares in an oil sands producer. KNOC pursued direct working interest position, with a partner than has the technological capabilities. Meanwhile other Asian countries had also shown interest in the oil sands, following the lead of Japan Canada Oil Sands Limited which is developing a C$ 150 mm project in northern Alberta to produce 10,000 bpd by 2005. The Hangingstone venture is owned 66.9% by state-owned Japan National Oil Corp., 6.2% by Japan Petroleum Exploration Co. and 26.9% by 70 Japanese companies.[14]

In July 2006 South Korea signed a deal to purchase a 100% stake in an oil sands mine in Canada that can produce 250 mm barrels of oil. It said the estimated size of the Blackgold Mine in the Cold Lake region of Alberta will allow South Korea to extract 30,000-35,000 barrels of oil per day for the next 25 years.

Hwang Doo-yul, CEO of state-run Korea National Oil Corp. (KNOC), and Geoff Waterman, vice president of Newmont Mining of Canada, signed the deal in Seoul. The Canadian company is an affiliate of US-based Newmont Mining Corp., the world's largest gold producer.

The South Korean firm was expected to begin production in 2008, with full-scale operations to commence two years later. KNOC paid $ 270 mm for the mining rights and expects annual sales to reach $ 500 mm once full-scale production commences. Oil sands, also referred to as tar or bituminous sands, are deposits of bitumen trapped in a mixture of clay, sand and water. They are in essence sand or sandstone containing at least 10% petroleum. There are estimated to be 175 bn barrels of petroleum that can be extracted from oil sands mines around the world, with Canada having the world's second-largest reserve of oil sands after Venezuela. Canada, which has most of its oil sands mines in the Peace River, Cold Lake and Athabasca regions of Alberta, can churn out 4.7 bn barrels of oil on an annual basis. The ministry said once production begins, the country's oil output self-sufficiency level could be raised by around 1.2%. South Korea currently produces 115,000 barrels of oil daily from local and overseas oil fields. Seoul wants to raise the self-sufficiency level from around 4% at present to 18% in 2013.[15]

In March 2008, Korea National Oil Corp. (KNOC) had let a contract to IMV Projects, part of John Wood Group, for front-end engineering and design of a 10,000-bpd heavy oil development in northern Alberta.

The steam-assisted gravity drainage project is on the Black-Gold oil sands lease, which KNOC acquired from Newmont Mining Corp. in August 2006. The 39-sq-km lease is 140 km southeast of Fort McMurray.

Through year end 2007, KNOC had drilled 18 holes for core analysis, acquired 23 sq km of 3D seismic data, and drilled two water-supply wells.

KNOC plans eventually to produce 30,000 bpd from the lease. It estimates BlackGold holds more than 200 mm bbl of recoverable bitumen.

Limitation of Canadian Oil Sands Developments

Recently, energy companies are cutting back development of Canadian oil sands, as crude prices plunge and processing costs become prohibitive. Royal Dutch Shell, the world's second-largest oil company, and Calgary-based Suncor Energy and EnCana stated that they would reduce plans to extract bitumen, the tar-like raw material for the crude, after prices fell 65% to $ 37.07 a barrel since July 4, 2008. The Canadian Association of Petroleum Producers also reduced its forecast for spending next year by 20% to C$ 16 bn ($ 13.6 bn).

Moreover, in June 2008, the trade group announced that companies would spend C$ 126 bn over the next five years on pipelines, mines and upgrading plants as record oil prices made the Canadian reserves in Alberta increasingly lucrative. The figure has now been chopped to about C$ 80 bn, Greg Stringham, a vice president at the association, said on Nov. 7, 2008. "Because of the economic uncertainty and turmoil that's out there right now, both the availability of capital and the lower pricing, people are waiting to see how long and how deep that is going to be,'' Stringham said.[16]

Companies can get oil from processing bitumen dug from mines or coaxed from the ground using steam. It takes two tons of oil sands to make one barrel of oil. Oil-sands projects will be profitable if crude is priced at $ 95 to $ 100 per barrel in coming decades. Bitumen can be tapped at existing projects for roughly $ 40 a barrel. The oil-sands oil typically tends to be the most expensive barrel to produce.[17]

Oil Demand Crunched

The Cold Lake blend must go through an upgrading process, adding C$ 20 to C$ 25 to the cost of the product that goes to refineries. Oil prices fell as the global credit crunch that forced financial companies to report $ 688 bn in losses and write-downs since the start of 2007 caused the world economy to slow. The cooling economy will cut global oil demand for the first time in a quarter of a century next year, Wood Mackenzie Consultants stated on Nov. 6. 2008. Oil demand in the US, the oil sands only export customer, will slump 830,000 bpd, or 4.3% this year from 2007 to 19.8 mm bpd, the Energy Department predicted Oct. 7.

EnCana cited financial market uncertainty on Oct. 15 when it delayed a plan to spin off Cenovus Energy, which was formed to manage oil-sands projects in Alberta and US refineries. Closely held Value Creation, based in Calgary, stopped work on a C$ 4 bn upgrader, which separates bitumen from sands and converts it to heavy oil, because of financing, Gerry Gabinet, director of economic development in Strathcona County Alberta where the upgrader was planned, said on Sept. 25, 2008.

EnCana, Imperial, Suncor

Oslo-based StatoilHydro, Norway's largest oil company, said August 11, 2008 that it may postpone the start of its oil-sands upgrader. Bruce March, chief executive officer for Imperial, which is 70%-owned by ExxonMobil, said Aug. 6 the company is deciding whether to proceed with the Kearl oil sands project, citing rising costs of development. Suncor announced on Oct. 23, 2008 it would cut back on construction at its Voyageur oil-sands project in Northern Alberta because of tumbling crude prices and will focus on another site. The same day, Petro-Canada and UTS Energy, based in Calgary said they may postpone an oil-sands processing facility near Edmonton. A week later, Shell said it would delay an investment decision on expanding its Athabasca oil-sands project because of construction costs. The company, based in The Hague, said it will press ahead with the first phase of the project.[18]

Environmental Problems

US policies that discourage fuel purchases from heavy-polluting sources are further reducing incentives to exploit oil sands. The crude creates three times more greenhouse gases than conventional wells, and a US law enacted in December bans federal agencies from buying fuels that cause more emissions than alternatives.

Oil-sands mines along the Athabasca River near Fort McMurray, Alberta, can be 80 meters (262 feet) deep and claimed almost 500 sq km (311 sq miles) of forest. They have created bitumen and clay-laden ponds with an oily sheen of grey and green hues that have killed scores of birds.

Oil sands hold the equivalent of 173 bn barrels, enough to supply the US for 24 years. Only Saudi Arabia has more crude. Producers are trying to get pipelines built that would take the oil to millions more consumers by allowing shipments to Asia and to the US Gulf Coast, home to 47% of the nation's refining capacity, according to US Energy Department data.

A line sponsored by Enbridge to the British Columbia coast may not be built before 2014, Pat Daniel, the company's chief executive officer, said in a conference call to analysts July 31. Two conduits to Texas cosponsored by Enbridge, one with

ExxonMobil and another with BP, won't be ready until 2012 at the earliest, Enbridge said in separate August statements.[19]

Implications

The oil sands still represent the largest investment opportunity in the global energy sector to date. Of the total proven reserves of 174 billion barrels, only 3% has been produced to date. In comparison, most oil producing regions are past their prime production periods and are facing declines in their conventional oil production.

Moreover, Canada and the province of Alberta have implemented investor friendly tax and royalty regimes to encourage the rapid development and exploitation of the oil sands resource. Despite massive investment and the four decades long development, only 20% of all oil sands leases have been acquired so far. This means that future investment chances for South Korean companies or government sectors are still immense. South Korea must bear in mind that Canada is one of the most geopolitically stable countries in the world and has existing trading relationships and closest proximity to the largest importer of oil. The majority of the world's excess oil production and reserves are in politically and economically unstable regions such as Caspian Sea, Middle East, or Africa.

Perhaps, besides oil sand issue, other possible energy cooperation between Canada and South Korea also include establishment of joint R&D type project on the environmentally sustainable renewable energy. In fact, renewable energy sources, such as wind, solar energy, bio mass are beginning to gain more attention as Canada works toward meeting international obligations to reduce greenhouse gas emissions. President Lee Myong Bak's Green Energy Revolution project and the Canadian experience for the strong existing infrastructure for renewable energy technology would be substantially a good mutual stepping stone to enhance further energy cooperation between the two countries.

NOTES

1. Energy Information Administration (EIA), on http: //www.eia.doe.gov/emeu/cabs/Canada/Background.html, accessed on 8 March 2009.
2. Energy Information Administration (EIA), Country Energy Analysis: Canada, 19 December 2002.
3. EIA, on http: //www.eia.doe.gov/cabs/Canada/Oil.html, accessed on 6 March 2009.
4. Energy Information Administration (EIA), Country Energy Analysis: Canada, 19 December 2002.
5. EIA, on http: //www.eia.doe.gov/cabs/Canada/Oil.html, accessed on 6 March 2009.
6. *Ibid.*
7. *Ibid.*
8. EIA, on http: //www.eia.doe.gov/cabs/Canada/Oil.html, accessed on 6 March 2009.
9. Gates, Derek S. The Canadian Oil Sands Investors' Guide (Victoria: Trafford Publishing, 2006), p. 11.
10. Alberta Energy: Oil Sands, on http: //www.energy.gov.ab.ca/oilsands/oilsands.asp, accessed on March 1, 2009.
11. *Ibid.*
12. Gates, pp. 28-29.
13. Gates, pp. 29-30.
14. "South Korea is looking to invest in Alberta's oil sands," Energy 24, March 20, 2001.
15. *The Korea Times*, July 27, 2006
16. Http: //www.bloomberg.com, Nov. 11, 2008
17. *Ibid.*
18. *Ibid.*
19. *Ibid.*

Prisoners Radio in Canada and Australia

HEATHER ANDERSON
Griffith University, Brisbane, Australia

Prejean:	Who are the good people listening on the other end of this program?
Interviewer:	Who's listening? Well, it's the prisoners' program, for people on the inside, prisoners.
Prejean:	It's *all* prisoners?
Interviewer:	And anyone else who wants to listen, usually just prisoners and their loved ones on the outside and we sort of keep a connection between them.
Prejean:	So they can all hear me?
Interviewer:	They will . . . yes, they will hear you.
Prejean:	Well, because, oh it's a privilege, it's a privilege to be able to be in sound of their hearts, and their ears, and themselves, and so I'm very, very happy to be doing this

(Interview with Sister Helen Prejean, *Locked In*, 14/3/05)

The above quote was taken from an interview conducted with Sister Helen Prejean for the Australian prisoners' radio show, *Locked In*, on Brisbane community radio station, 4ZzZ. Sister Prejean is a Roman Catholic nun and a leading advocate for the abolition of the death penalty. She has acted as a spiritual adviser to many prisoners on death row, witnessing a number of their executions. Sister Prejean wrote a book about these experiences—*Dead Man Walking*—which was nominated for a Pulitzer and became the basis of an Academy Award winning film of the same name, in which Susan Sarandon played her role.

Sister Prejean's surprise (and joy) at being interviewed for a prisoners' radio program demonstrates the underground nature of the genre. While there are a handful of prisoners' radio shows in the United States, where she is from, the concept of a broadcast dedicated to the incarcerated was unheard of by Prejean. This is not unexpected. Prisoners' radio hardly registers on the radar, not only in the spheres of prison advocacy, but also in academic circles and community radio sectors worldwide.

My thesis addresses the current lack of information about prisoners' radio programming. I examine prisoners' radio as a collective case study, in that the genre itself is examined. Further data was gathered via four detailed case studies of specific programs: *Stark Raven* at Coop Radio, Vancouver, Canada; Prisoners' Justice Day programming at CKUT, Montreal, Canada; 4ZzZ, *Locked In* at Brisbane, Australia; and *Beyond the Bars* at 3CR, Melbourne, Australia. I employ a dual framework for analysing my case studies that includes both producers and audiences as active agents. I argue that this diverse approach is necessary to fully appreciate the functions of prisoners' radio.

I have chosen to use the word "prisoner" as opposed to "inmate" throughout my research. This is informed by Canadian prison activist, Claire Culhane (1988), who says "inmate" is a label that creates a sense of institutionalisation and powerlessness. The preferred term, "prisoner," is more accurate as it alludes to those who are "temporarily deprived of freedom and liberty, held captive" (Culhane 1988: 20). Similarly, I prefer "prisons" to the plethora of terms now used to refer to places of incarceration (such as correctional facilities, reception centres and institutions) which serve to "camouflage their restrictive and secretive role" (Culhane 1988: 20).

About the researcher

Before the commencement of my Ph.D. research, I had never been officially connected to a prisoners' program. I have, however, been a volunteer at 4ZzZ in Brisbane, Australia since 1990 and contributed many prison-related news stories and documentaries for broadcast and acted as a "back-up" announcer for regular prisoner show presenters, a number of whom were my friends as well as colleagues. One of these, Nicki Debreczeni, was presenting *Locked In* on her own when I decided to offer my services as a volunteer during my Ph.D. The insights given to me through this hands-on participation allowed me to gather rich data, and, more importantly, to develop a more thorough understanding of the genre itself, so as to apply this to my other, more remote, case study choices.

What is Prisoners' Radio?

Defining prisoners' radio is not a simple undertaking. Each program has its own format. However, broadly speaking there are two distinct types of prisoners' show: those that mainly play requests and dedications and those that primarily focus on providing information about prison issues. Just to complicate matters, it is also quite common for such shows to act as a hybrid of sorts, incorporating both information and requests to varying degrees. Internationally, radio that operates for, or by, prisoners exists almost exclusively within the community radio context.

An all-inclusive definition of prisoners' radio would include at least some of the following elements: news stories, interviews, documentaries and other information that relates to prison and justice issues; song requests to and from prisoners, their families and friends, often with accompanying personal messages; and broadcasting from either inside a detention centre or working with inmates to produce their own radio pieces. Prisoners' radio can involve prisoners, former prisoners, their friends and family, social justice activists and/ or government representatives as well as community radio broadcasters and the occasional prison staff member.

As I said earlier, little has been documented about this type of community radio process and practice. Programs tend to exist unbeknown to one another and any links between them are generally developed through personal relationships as opposed to any formal networking. This being said, the primary intention of my research was to examine prisoners' radio on a deeper level than merely cataloguing and describing it. I was interested in their major strengths and weaknesses of and how these successes or limitations could be measured. By what means can we evaluate prisoners' radio? These issues became pivotal to my research.

Theoretical Framework Development

Prisoners' media is a sub-genre of community radio programming in general and, as such, contemporary theoretical understandings of alternative media—and community radio specifically—are a logical and appropriate springboard for its theorisation. One framework that I find particularly relevant to community radio is the citizens' media model developed by Clemencia Rodriguez (2001). Community radio is a participatory venture, legislated to involve local communities in both production and management. Citizens' media focuses on this participation and the effects it has on those involved and, through this, radio-making becomes an act of citizenship—of actively contributing to society. Emphasis is placed on what this participation "does" or "means" to those involved.

I was particularly attracted to the notion of applying citizens' media theory to the prisoner population. Generally speaking, prisoners have been stripped of their citizenship status or identity. Legally, many prisoners are not allowed to vote, and in some countries disenfranchisement is permanent, even after prisoners have completed their full sentences. Still, in nations where prisoners do retain their right to vote, incarceration limits the ability to fully enact this right and radical democratic theory (on which citizens' media is heavily based) emphasises the broader definitions of citizenship beyond that of those legally bestowed.

Limiting the ability to participate in society—or enact citizenship—may be one of the reasons behind incarceration. However, the reality is that the vast majority of prisoners are serving short sentences and will return to their communities after release. High recidivism rates across the world indicate that "something is amiss" with current models of punishment. Prisons do not diminish the crime rate but rather promote recidivism, and cannot fail but produce delinquents (Foucault 1995). Could it be that the temporary extinguishment of prisoners' citizenship is hindering the reintegration of prisoners into society? Are there means by which prisoners can retain some sense of active citizenship or connection to community, during times of legal exclusion, that may be beneficial in the long term?

It is at this point that I have to "pull in the reins" and note that I have no background in criminology or criminal psychology. It was at a similar point during the development of my research question that I realised I needed to define the scope, or boundaries, of my study. Was I equipped to enter into the fields of rehabilitation, restitution and punishment? At what moment would I be out of my depth?

I decided that the main focus of my research was the media themselves and there was "enough" to learn about what prisoners' media was "doing" without attempting a detailed study of "how" these actions were affecting prisoner behaviour or long term attitudes. While I was very interested in what prisoners had to say about the programs, and what they felt the shows achieved, I was not in a position to monitor effects over a prolonged period of time. In essence, my goal was to research prisoners' radio, not prisoners themselves.

Armed with what I felt was a strong theoretical argument linking citizens' media and prisoners' radio, I was faced with a new dilemma—where did the wider audience fit in? Prisoners are not the only people "using" prisoners' radio, as listeners or participants. What about the advocate groups who promote their issues and events on such shows, or the friends and family members who use them to communicate with their loved ones, and even the general audience who listen purely out of interest or enjoyment? These communities of interest all "use" prisoners' radio to varying degrees—and while I had made an explicit decision to not concentrate on rehabilitation as such, tenuous connections can be made between the "inclusion of community" and prisoners' wellbeing.

Many prisoners' radio programs focus on the dissemination of news and information about prison-related issues, rather than the direct participation of prisoners. Two complimentary, yet distinct, functions of prisoners' radio began to emerge in my research and neither could be sufficiently explained, or examined, within the confines of citizens' media. Such a framework did not adequately recognise the work achieved by these information-based programs and so I turned to ideas emerging in theorising alternative media and public sphere, which I felt more adequately acknowledges the contributions prisoners' radio make in fostering a wider understanding of prisoner's issues. This way I could consider the benefits and barriers, not only for the prisoners who participated, but also for the full spectrum of listeners. By considering prisoners' programming within a public sphere discourse, I could fill in "the gaps" and develop a deeper understanding than could be achieved by applying a citizens' media framework alone.

Descriptions of the Case Studies

Stark Raven, Co-op Radio, CFRO, Vancouver, British Columbia, Canada

Stark Raven's format emulates a traditional current affairs program with theme music, defined segments (news headlines and community announcements) and similar introductions and conclusions. This being said, the politics of the program are considerably more radical than the "typical" current affairs program. *Stark Raven* acts as a form of social movement media by focusing on critical analysis and local community events. The show usually broadcasts two or three in-depth stories per program and a wide range of topics relating to criminalisation are discussed.

Stark Raven is also re-broadcast on another community radio station in Canada, as well as being podcast and made available on activist websites. Heavier emphasis is placed on disseminating alternative dialogue about prison issues to a wider audience than providing a local service for prisoners themselves.

Locked In, 4ZzZ, Brisbane, Queensland, Australia

Locked In is a program that relies heavily on its prisoner audience to provide much of its content and direction. While the show does include some news and information, this is secondary to prisoners' letters and phone calls from friends and family. *Locked In* also changes over time, and an increase in volunteers who had experienced incarceration themselves led to direct increase in prisoners' engagement with the program. These changes would not have been documented if my research had not been conducted over two separate time periods.

Listeners' incentives to participate changed over time. While messages dominated both samples, in 2005 the main target of these messages were loved ones on the outside, whereas in 2007 this changed to messages to other prisoners, usually in the form of "gigging." Prisoners' engagement in the program increased significantly in 2007 with the addition of three former prisoners to the *Locked In* team and there is evidence that prisoners felt a heightened sense of ownership with the program's 2007 format.

Prisoners' Justice Day Programming, CKUT, Montreal, Quebec, Canada

Prisoners' Justice Day is commemorated in Canada on August 10, each year. While I outline the programming on a national scale, my focus is on the broadcasting of one station—CKUT in Montreal. CKUT's Prisoners' Justice Day programming speaks volumes about the radio station itself. The dedication of large portions of "regular" broadcast time to prisoners' issues demonstrates a high commitment to social justice issues. The treatment is in-depth, covering a wide range of issues and giving voice to various communities and groups of people. The scope of Prisoners' Justice Day programming across Canada has the potential to grow considerably with the introduction of CKUT's national syndication.

Stark Raven and CKUT both talk to a broader audience than *Locked In* and *Beyond the Bars*, my two Australian examples, programs that ultimately appeal to a much narrower group of listeners. Academics, activists, lawyers, support workers and journalists from diverse backgrounds and (inter-connecting) communities are represented in the programs. While the voices of prisoners do appear, they are far less prominent than in the Australian case-studies. On the other hand, *Locked In* and *Beyond the Bars* spend significantly less time exploring the issues of criminalisation and the conditions within prisons themselves, especially in relation to immigration detention centres, military camps and the wider arena of legislative and enforcement developments in the wake of September 11.

Beyond the Bars, 3CR, Melbourne, Victoria, Australia

Beyond the Bars is an annual event that works directly with Indigenous prisoners to produce content for broadcast. The results of these workshops are two-fold—a series of broadcasts from inside prison during NAIDOC Week (two of which are conducted live from inside prison) and a CD. *Beyond the Bars* engages prisoners' participation more directly than any of the other case studies in my research. The broadcasts primarily comprise of creative works (often developed in preparatory workshops), messages to loved ones along with best wishes for those celebrating NAIDOC week, and political and personal discussions—all of which add a highly personal element to the broadcasts.

The 2007 *Beyond the Bars* programs were more arts-based than discussion-based with creative works dominating the broadcasts. This could be explained by the maturity of the project. Recurring themes are the desire to improve situations, loss and survival of culture, drugs and love. There is one final element of the *Beyond the Bars* broadcasts that applies equally to both time periods—the extremely personal nature of both the content and the presentation style. Prisoners speak candidly about their lives, their offences and their plans for the future while relationships between broadcasters and participants are openly familiar.

Concluding Remarks

What my research found was that my initial "ideas" were pretty much correct—there are two major, and complementary, roles of prisoners' radio—the first relating to information, while the second more participatory in nature. What was interesting was that my Canadian case studies reflected the second of these—the public sphere model, while the Australian examples reflected the first—a participatory model. This data cannot, however, be extrapolated to claim one country focuses on prisoner participation while another targets prison news and analysis—for example the Canadian *Souverains Anonymes* is by far the most participatory driven prisoners' program I have discovered—while shows such as *Doing Time* and *Jailbreak* in Australia are predominantly information based. The data does however reflect the dual purpose of prisoners' radio—direct participation and facilitating wider public sphere discussion of prison issues—and opens many avenues for future research.

References

Culhane, Claire. 1988, *Still Barred from Prison: Social Injustice in Canada*, 3rd Volume, Black Rose Books, Montreal.

Locked in 2005, Broadcast, March 14, 2005.

Foucault, Michel. 1995, *Discipline and Punish: The Birth of the Prison*, trans. Alan Sheridan, Vintage Books, New York.

Rodriguez, Clemencia. 2001, *Fissures in the Mediascape—An International Study of Citizens' Media*, Hampton Press, New Jersey.

Policing Multicultural States: Lessons from the Canadian Model

GUY BEN-PORAT
Department of Public Policy and Administration
Ben-Gurion University of the Negev, Israel

Policing is a controversial issue in diverse societies where cultures, religions and competing national identities challenge the existing order, and where the police have yet to develop the capabilities to engage with diversity and overcome its own biases and prejudices. The discussion of policing in multicultural society is embedded in a wider context of political responses to diversity. However, the issue of policing is salient because of the nature of police work and the type of engagement it entails. Minority groups may be alienated from the police they perceive as enforcing unjust and discriminating policies or because of language and cultural barriers. These perceptions can, on the one hand, undermine police work and, on the other hand, prevent minority groups from receiving the police services they need. These difficulties are especially acute where police and minorities have a history of violence that underscores high levels of mutual mistrust. The tense relation observed in different countries between police and minorities is a public policy dilemma where police debates its effectiveness against its legitimacy and its organizational structure and culture against the changes of a multicultural society that press for reform.

The purpose of this work is to explore the difficulties of policing in multicultural states, study the challenges of police reform and outline a model of multicultural policing based upon the Canadian experience.[1] While many democratic states debate their multicultural character and implement multicultural policies at different levels, Canada is unique in formally adopting a multicultural identity. This multicultural identity was translated into different policies and provides Canada with a comprehensive policy experience in various issues, including policing. Consequently, police reforms in Canada engage not with neo-liberal cuts of spending and new modes of governance (Lithopoulos and Rigakos, 2005) or with "rationalization" of police services (Murphy, 2004) but also reforms that aim to improve the police's credibility and legitimacy among ethnic minorities.

Police credibility and legitimacy among minorities is yet to be fully achieved in Canada as visible minorities feel they are treated unfairly by the police. Relations between police and certain visible minorities are greatly over-represented in the criminal court system (especially in Ontario) and that black people believe that the police treats members of their racial group worst than they do white people so that they are more likely to be unfairly stopped and questioned by the police (Wortley, 2003). The widespread public belief that the police engage in racial profiling was perceived a significant threat to the ability of the police to maintain public order and ensure public safety, even if the actual proof of racial profiling remained inconclusive (Melchers, 2003). The dissatisfaction of minority groups and at times their distrust of the police, on the one hand, and the overarching commitment to multiculturalism, on the other hand, underscore initiatives for reform in police services in Canada. The Canadian experience is not one of complete success but rather an ongoing debate over various reforms this research will draw upon.

This research is the outcome of documents collected and interviews conducted with police officers in Ontario, it is designed to understand the problems of multicultural policing and the strategies employed to meet these challenges. While Ontario is one of Canada's thirteen provinces and variations are likely between them its engagement with policing vis-à-vis the commitment to multiculturalism is a significant part of the Canadian experience. Moreover, it is the largest police force in terms of spending and number of police officers. Consequently, the study of this experience provides a framework for understanding the problems and solutions that the policing of multicultural states requires. Interviewees for this research were approached formally through several police organizations in Ontario and were representatives of the Toronto Police, Ottawa Police, Kingston Police, the RCMP and Ministry of Community Safety and Correctional Services. During the in-depth interviews they were requested to identify the main challenges of multicultural policing, describe initiatives and provide their personal experience and views of police reforms taken. Documents and policy papers were collected in the different agencies visited. Finally, interviews were conducted also with two civil rights organizations, the *Canadian Race Relations Foundation* and the *Urban Alliance on Race Relations* to gain some understanding of minority perceptions of police and police reforms.

The next, theoretical, section will delineate the relations between multiculturalism, public policy and police reform and will be followed by a more focused debate on the contemporary challenges the multicultural reality presents for police forces and the often tense relations between police and minorities. The Canadian multicultural experience will be described in the next section and the evolvement of the debate over policing and police reforms. Finally, the three specific areas identified as central for police reforms and the dilemmas they entail will be described and analyzed: (a) recruitment and retention (b) practices of engagement with minority groups and their specific needs and (c) the abilities of communities to influence policing and related policy-making.

Multiculturalism, Public Policy and Police Reform

Cultural diversity and ethno-national politics are common to most contemporary states who, contrary to their image of homogeneity, must contend with a multicultural and, at times, multinational reality (Connor, 1994; Tully, 2002; Walker, 1994). Different perceptions of government, police, the law, appropriate social order, justice, child-rearing and different religious and cultural practices common to multicultural societies present major challenges for state institutions in general and for policing in particular (Stenning, 2003). Conflicts between minorities and the state can erupt for various reasons—economic, cultural or political—and it is the police who find themselves in the front line. The escalation of violence in some cases indicates that the state and the police are ill prepared for the task (Stenning, 2003). In other cases, it is the over-reaction of the police, underscored by its prejudices, that results in tragic consequences and further erodes the relations between the police and minorities. For example, the Israeli police shooting of 13 Palestinian citizens during demonstrations in October 2000 further eroded the trust of the Palestinian minority in the police and the state. Or, the beating of Rodney King, an African-American by the Los-Angeles police became a symbol of police brutality against minorities.

Policing has become a major source of concern for democratic countries with a diverse population, especially when relations between minorities and the state become tense and when "security concerns," real or imagined, erode tolerance towards minorities. These tensions can lead to mutually reinforcing negative perceptions between the police and minorities and outbursts of violence. Police reform, while necessary, is often a long and arduous process related to the nature of the police and its modes of operation. The police are regarded as a bureaucratic organization with paramilitary overtones characterized by a central command, hierarchy, complex division of labour, the impersonal enforcement of formal rules and the provision of rationally based services (Fleras, 1992: 116). Yet, police organizations function in a political context because they operate in a political arena and their mandate is defined politically (Manning, 2006). Accordingly, the modes of operation of police forces change across time and place so they reflect the state and society within which they operate. Police managers formulate goals and design organizations to meet the expectations and needs of elected politicians, employees, clients and other individuals and groups affected by police activities.

Reforms of the police in the early 20th century sought to professionalize the police, create uniform standards and make it effective in fighting crime so the police would be more accountable and predictable in its delivery of services (Roberg, Kuykendall and Novak, 2002: 49). This policy, based upon impersonal policing, has often led to the isolation of the police from society and, even more so, from minority groups who felt alienated from the police. Since the 1970s, the police in various democratic states have changed their strategy in order to gain legitimacy from society and to fight rising crime. The 'broken windows' approach advocated a zero-tolerance strategy for disorderly behaviour, in the belief that it would reduce crime. Police, according to this strategy, were to prevent "criminogenic conditions from developing, by isolating problems in their early manifestations and by creating strategies for eliminating them" (Herbert, 2006: 171). This strategy brought the police back into some communities. A focus on the external dangers to the community enhanced the role and authority of the police. Accordingly, this approach was often supported by middle class residents but raised objections among disadvantaged groups.

The 'broken windows' policy dovetailed well with the neoliberal climate in the US and the emphasis on fighting crime instead of promoting welfare, so minority groups were defined as dangerous rather than disadvantaged. Naturally, this strategy was often detrimental to relations between the policy and minority groups. "To ardently mandate that officers acquire more and more arrests is to invite them to cast suspicion on those who do not warrant it and abuse those who should be left alone. Such suspicion will invariably fall disproportionately on minority citizens, and thus further inflame already tense police-community relations in minority-dominated neighbourhoods" (Herbert, 2006: 183). This type of community engagement did not change many of the negative perceptions of minorities about the police. Rather, these policies served police "clients," the law-abiding citizens, who shared the police notion of public order, but alienated the marginalized, the ethnically and racially diverse, or the "troublemakers" (Findlay, 2004: 34 see also: Williams and Murphy, 2006).

Where countries are changing and diversifying, the police are likely to be aligned with the old cultural, economic and ethnic guard, or may be perceived as such by other constituents (Erez, Finckenauer and Ibarra, 2003). The recognition that the police must pay attention to the multicultural reality included the broadening of police functions from maintaining order to engaging in conflict resolution and problem solving, and providing services and activities that strengthen the link between the police and communities (Kelling and Moore, 2006). This approach examined, on the one hand, the history, culture, and current needs of minority groups and, on the other hand, often more reluctantly, the mode of operation of the police itself vis-à-vis minority groups. The latter included the assessment of "cultural sensitivity" or, in more extreme cases, "police racism" (Chan, 1997: 17). Consequently, the great challenge for police organizations at the turn of the twentieth century is to achieve legitimacy and credibility and the cooperation of minorities hitherto alienated from the police.

Engaging Multiculturalism

Demands for police reform received heightened attention when police biases towards minorities were exposed in "shocking" incidents or when events suggested that the police did not have the capacity to deal with the social tensions that are part of the multicultural reality. In the United Kingdom, for example, the murder of Stephen Lawrence, a young black man, by a racist group and the subsequent police mistreatment of the family exposed racism within the police and led to an inquiry committee and, later, to a debate over British multiculturalism and of "The future of multi-ethnic Britain" (Runnymede, 2000). In the United States, the beating of Rodney King by the Los Angeles Police led to a heated public discussion over the mistreatment of African Americans by the police. Racial and ethnic minorities, it was demonstrated, are more likely than white Americans to be arrested, stopped, questioned and searched by the police (Walker, Spohn and Delone, 2000).

The need for police reform was also acknowledged in Europe as the Office of the High Commissioner on National Minorities published a set of recommendations for policing multi-ethnic societies, a result of the absence, in some states, of institutional mechanisms to support the interaction and co-operation between police and national minorities (www.osce.org/hcnm/). Alternatively, police reform is part of a comprehensive process of post-conflict institution building. The Good Friday Agreement in Northern Ireland, for example, emphasized that "policing structures and arrangements are such that the police service is professional, effective and efficient, fair and impartial, free from partisan political control; accountable, both under the rule of law for its actions and to the community it serves." Indeed, the RUC in Northern Ireland is an example of a police force held illegitimate by one community, the Catholics, because from its inception it was charged not only with ordinary police duties but also with defending the Union (McGarry and Oleary, 1999). In the 1990s, the demand for police reforms was a major part of the peace process and one of the more sensitive issues that had to be resolved. The Independent Commission on Policing in Northern Ireland was set up as part of the Agreement reached in Belfast on 10 April 1998 and, following its recommendations, the RUC has changed to the *Police Service of Northern Ireland* with a new badge and new uniform.

The problems of police-minority relations can be defined as "under-policing" and/ or "over-policing" that combined or separately underscore the police's lack of legitimacy among minority groups. Over-policing implies mistreatment of minorities by the police, either by excessive use of force towards minorities or by discriminatory practices against them that include excessive routine use of "stop and search" and disproportionate arrest rates. Over-policing is often embedded in "cop culture" that includes moral and political conservatism related to prejudiced attitudes towards minorities, a siege mentality of "us against them" and resistance to change and reforms (Findlay, 2004: 101). Negative attitudes towards minorities often turn into self-fulfilling prophecies through actual encounters in poor minority neighbourhoods and underpin practices of "racial profiling," the targeting of persons or groups by the police on suspicion of criminal activity based primarily on race, ethnicity or other identifiable marks (www.crr.ca). Thus, the connections between social disadvantage and over-policing are strengthened by selective law enforcement stimulated by discriminatory police stereotyping (Findlay, 2004: 105). The stereotyping and discrimination that exist in routine police work can be compounded by the impact of (even a small minority of) true racists in the police force that "creates a vicious cycle that militates against good relationships between police and minorities" (Casey, 2000: 166).

Under-policing is largely about police neglect of minorities and their needs. Thus, complaints of racial harassment and attacks against minorities by racist groups can be ignored or not taken seriously. More common is the absence of police from minority neighbourhoods regarded as "hopeless" and the attempts to contain crime within the neighbourhood rather than make it a safe place for those who live in it. Thus, poor urban communities suffer from unresponsive policing and high crime rates. Finally, under-policing is apparent with respect to domestic violence characterized as "cultural" and ignored by the police because they believe that such crimes are normative in these communities (Brunson and Miller, 2006). The duality of over and under-policing implies that in minority neighbourhoods, there is limited or a complete lack of police presence or the police engage in violent and aggressive attempts to control crime. Minority groups are consequently torn between their fear of the police because of historic abuse and their desire for police protection from criminal elements that are disproportionately present in their communities (Howell, Perry and Vile, 2004).

Paradoxically, visible minorities can be inflicted with both under-policing and over-policing, suffer from crime in their neighbourhoods and from being stopped as suspects of crime outside of them. As a result, these minorities may have low trust in the police and be reluctant to cooperate with the police. Recommendations for police reforms related to multiculturalism and minority groups usually fall into six categories: (1) diversification of human resources; (2) cultural sensitivity training for police officers; (3) formal anti-racism policies within the police; (4) review and revision of operational practices that may lead to "systemic discrimination;" (5) liaison between the police and minority communities; and (6) inclusion of minority group representatives within the membership of the police's governing authorities (Stenning, 2003). These recommendations can be divided into three central areas that together tackle the central issues of over-policing and under-policing: the patterns of recruitment and training of police officers, revisions of police practices, and relations between police and communities.

The police force may not be representative of society or even homogeneous in terms of ethnicity, gender and class. Consequently, it tends to respond in predictable ways to situations because of common heritage, interests and training. In Canada, police officers referred to the old police service as largely composed of white males, a police force that had various difficulties, described below, to perform in the changing Canadian society. In more troubled areas like Israel and Northern Ireland very few, respectively, Arabs and Catholics were recruited to the police. Homogeneity can lead to a "police subculture" that is usually influenced by the dominant societal culture and, consequently discriminates against and marginalizes minorities regarded alien and suspicious. The diversification of the police force, therefore, is an important step in police reform. However, because the police subculture is characterized by a distinctive ideology, norms and values, it can be maintained through the assimilation of new recruits so that changes in recruitment patterns will have a limited influence (Desroches, 1992). Training police officers to be culturally sensitive is central, therefore, to changing police attitudes and perceptions.

The measures of diversity and training have to be accompanied by actual changes in policy regarding the interaction between police and minorities and measured by the change in how the police operate on the streets. In order to gain legitimacy and the trust of minority groups, the police have to uproot prejudices and discriminatory practices in both under-policing and over-policing. These measures, however, have to be properly implemented and continuously assessed in order to determine their effect. Without the monitoring and review, the police may be tempted to just "go through the motions," so that the gulf between them and the minority communities will not be bridged.

Finally, institutional changes in police-community relations are also part of the reform because they provide formal and informal channels for communities to convey their needs and concerns. This reform includes the involvement of the communities in everyday police work, in policy-making deliberations and in overseeing police work. Community policing includes principles, policies, and practices that link police and community members together in the joint pursuit of local crime prevention (Fleras, 1992: 74). It is based on a decentralization of authority and decision-making processes, neighbourhood focus and community input, accountability, partnership, community-based consultation and a general shift from criminal law enforcement toward social service, community problem solving and crime prevention (Roberg, Kuykendall and Novak, 2002: 56). Combined, the measures of recruitment and training of police officers, reform of discriminatory practices of policing and the involvement of the community itself in policing, designing policy and oversight, underscore police reform and adaptation to a multicultural setting.

The Canadian Context

In the adoption of multiculturalism in 1971 and its formalization in the multiculturalism act (1985) the Canadian government declared that its policy is to "recognize and promote the understanding that multiculturalism reflects the cultural and racial diversity of Canadian society and acknowledges the freedom of all members of Canadian society to preserve, enhance and share their cultural heritage" (http: //www.canadian heritage.gc.ca/progs/multi/policy/act_e.cfm). Multicultural policy had four aims: to support the cultural development of ethnocultural groups, to allow members of these groups full participation in Canadian society, to promote encounters and interchange among ethnocultural groups and to assist new immigrants in acquiring at least one of Canada's official languages (Kymlicka, 1998: 15). As a policy, therefore, multiculturalism includes federal, provincial and municipal commitments to cultural diversity in order to accommodate the needs of different groups and provide culturally sensitive public services (Troper and Weinfeld, 1999: 11-13).

Police departments in Canada began in the 1980s to debate how to improve their image among disaffected constituents and minority groups. Canadian police were criticized for discrimination, stereotypes and insensitivity, alienation from their clients, a militaristic subculture and structure, the under-representation of minorities and inadequate grievance procedures for victims of police mistreatment (Fleras, 1992: 92-3). While in the past the police might have been able to ignore the complaints of First Nations' people and ethnic minorities, due to their relatively small numbers, the flood of immigration from non-Western countries in the 1980s, described as a "demographic revolution," demanded a new approach. "We are witnessing nothing short of a demographic revolution following the influx of immigrants and refugees from Third World countries . . . the experiences, perceptions, and expectations that newcomers bring with them to Canada puts an additional burden on the police in coping with the demands of diverse constituents" (Cryderman, O'toole and Fleras, 1992: vii).

The events following the 9/11 terrorist attacks were a grim reminder of the need to adapt to diversity. Muslim citizens, on the one hand, complained they were harassed and the police, on the other hand, realized they had a limited ability to engage with these communities. Consequently, the police decided that they had "to outreach all the diverse communities of Canada because the protection of national security needs the awareness and involvement of all citizens" (RCMP Internal document, 2006). According to Alok Mukherjee, the Chair of Toronto Police Service Board, there was another aspect to this outreach, human resources. Expecting large retirements in coming years, the police would have to compete for talent among a labour force made up of immigrants. Diversity, therefore, will matter both inside the organization and with the communities the police will serve, so there are business reasons for addressing diversity, something the private sector, a competitor for human resources, is already doing (Mukherjee, Interview).

The Canadian police are arguably at the forefront of engagement with the changing make-up of Canadian society in its comprehensive range of contacts with individuals and communities that requires openmindedness and adaptability, some claim the police have yet to achieve. Racial minorities, as well as the gay community, complain that their communities are over-policed, misrepresented within the police organization and discriminated against in police practices. "Citizens who belong to these groups believe that the police have placed them in a category of "other" which deserves less respect and is granted less status, fewer rights, and more obligations" (Ungerleider, 1994). Suspicion of the police is exacerbated in some cases by immigrants' negative perceptions about and experience with the police in their home countries where the latter are associated with oppressive political regimes, the arbitrary use of power, and corruption.

Another source of tension is the struggle of marginalized groups against society and the state, a struggle in which the police are called upon to intervene to "restore order." Indigenous people, for example, fight through political, legal, or extra-legal means to regain lands, social rights and recognition. When these struggles escalate into confrontations, the police, as an arm of government, are at the forefront. Minority and Indigenous communities are often socially, politically and economically marginalized and disadvantaged, suffer from less education, high unemployment and, consequently, are over-represented in most facets of the justice system. In the end, "in most communities it is usually the police who are called upon to deal with fruits of social, political and economic neglect" (Loree, 2001). Prejudice within the police is strengthened by the negative experience of encounters with minorities, creating a vicious cycle between the police and minority communities.

Several inquiries and commissions regarding discrimination and racism have supported many of the claims made against the police. The Race Relations and Policing Task Force in 1989 clearly stated, "Public approval will be the result of visible and credible efforts by police to assess the nature and degree of racism in police forces. If the police are seen to eliminate organizational factors which perpetuate prejudice and to punish discriminatory behaviour they will be assured of public confidence." The Task Force made 57 recommendations that included increasing the representation of visible minorities in the police services and improving community relations. The Ontario Police Service Act was introduced in 1990 as an attempt to reform the police and strengthen its relations with the communities. The justice system, as well as the police, seemed to suffer from biases and are therefore perceived by minorities unfair. A *Report of the Commission on Systemic Racism in the Ontario Criminal Justice System* of 1995 stated, "Commission findings leave no doubt that the system is experienced as unfair by racialized people and, at key points in the administration of justice, the exercise of discretion has a harsher impact on black than white people. The conclusion is inescapable: the criminal justice system tolerates racialization in its practices."

The negative engagements of visible minorities, aboriginals and gay people with the police led to wide criticism of its practices. The Canadian Race Relations Foundation found that the efforts of the police fell short of what communities expected. "Most communities want the police to root out crimes . . . people would want that to happen. [but] They want also that the police would not be racist and mistreat minorities and that racist policemen would be rooted out. You want to see that a professional police takes on these issues but in many cases the police tend to protect their own, and because of the system they enjoy more than others the benefit of the doubt" (Yep and Hunter, Interview). Similarly, the Urban Alliance on Race Relations challenged the police not to place the blame on a "few bad apples" but to seriously reflect on changes necessary.

These complaints were not accepted by the police at face value but police officials recognized the need for reforms and have implemented various plans to address the grievances of minority groups. Police reform, according to senior personnel interviewed, is, on the one hand, the result of a critique of police operations and charges of insensitivity or racism and, on the other hand, a growing recognition that cultural sensitivity and community outreach will create a better police force. The implementation of diversity as part of police reforms is essentially about ending over-policing and under-policing and making the police more acceptable to all communities. The Canadian federal system and internal diversity imply that different initiatives are carried out because the administration of justice is the responsibility of the provinces as well as the Royal Canadian Mounted

Police (RCMP), which, as a national police service, provides policing services under contract to eight provinces and three territories. Even among the sites chosen for this research within the Province of Ontario—Toronto, Kingston, Ottawa and the RCMP—attitudes and policies varied. Thus, as examined below, questions of recruitment, retention, training, community engagement and practices yield different answers and solutions.

It is recognized, therefore, that minority groups in Canada suffer from a combination of under-policing and over-policing. Reform, consequently, will be examined in this work in the context of the three issues identified as central to the relations between the police and minority groups—the measures of recruitment and training of police officers, reform of discriminatory practices of policing and the involvement of the community itself in policing.

Recruitment, Retention and Training

Police in multicultural societies have to make an effort in recruitment in order to make the police reflective of society at large. However, there are practical and environmental difficulties that include the educational levels of immigrants and minorities and intangible aspects of attitudes on both sides (Casey, 2000). Sectors within the police might express their "concerns" over the lowering of standards for minority applicants, often an expression of their own biases. Minorities, for their part, might not regard policing as a desirable or respectable career and in more extreme cases may even portray those among them who join the force as "traitors." Such attitudes raise a first set of questions about how minorities are approached, what goals are set for recruitment and how are they measured. A second set of questions involves the roles minority recruits are assigned to, the police culture towards minority recruits, and the retention and promotion potential of minorities in the police force.

The attempts to diversify the police workforce were meant not only to follow the *Employment Equity Act* that intends to "correct the conditions of disadvantage in employment experienced by women, aboriginal peoples, persons with disabilities and members of visible minorities" (http: //laws.justice.gc.ca /en/ShowFullDoc/cs/E-5.401///en) but also to improve police performance. Police services in Canada are beginning to understand that they need to be an employer of choice, so they have to present themselves as part of society and diversify the police force (Interview, David Snoddy, Ministry of Community Safety and Correctional Services, Ontario). Recruitment of minorities involves making the police an attractive and respectable profession for minority groups and overcoming existing suspicions (Yuen, Beahan, Bevan interviews). These suspicions are the result either of immigrants' experiences in their home country or of minority groups' negative perception of the police. People who join the police from these groups may be viewed negatively by the communities, at times described by the derogatory terms "Oreo" for a black police officer (black on the outside, white on the inside) and "apple" for an aboriginal police officer (red on the outside, white on the inside).

The Toronto Police set goals for 2006 to achieve the status of an employer of choice and to increase recruitment from identified groups (women, visible minority, aboriginal, disability, sexual orientation and people who speak more than one language). These goals were translated into specific objectives of a formal "Relationship Management" and a pre-defined number of recruits, representative of the city's demographics, so that an average of 40 percent diversity will be achieved in the graduating classes of recruits (Yuen, Interview). Statistics collected in 2007 find that among uniform police racial minorities occupy 9.3 percent of the senior positions, 7.7 percent of staff sergeants and 17.3 percent of constables and a total of 15.6 percent of the uniform employee. Aboriginals occupy none of the senior positions, 0.4 percent of staff sergeants and 1.1 percent of constables and a total of 1 percent of the uniform employee (Employment Statistics, Toronto Police Services).

In the RCMP, targets for recruitment were also made, and the diversity of the police force is considered a significant benefit. "Once you get into a room with diverse people you realize that your little world is just your little world . . . everybody has equal if not greater value to add . . . you get exposed to things you would never think would effect or implicate you of because they are not in your normal way of thinking" (Interview, Macaulay). In the Ottawa police, until not long ago, about 90 percent of the new recruits were white males, but in recent years, they have constituted only 50 percent or less of the class. The police also use community activists for recruiting from communities previously closed to the police (Interview, Bevan). Several years ago, the Ottawa police began to conduct an internal census among its workforce in order to identify the demographic characteristics of its employees. The survey, voluntary and anonymous, asked not only about visible characteristics but also about less visible (or even invisible ones) like religion and sexual orientation and cultural groups of relatives. The results of the survey, in which 73 percent of employees participated, were to be used in police recruitment so that the police force would be reflective of the society it serves.

Efforts to diversify have to take into account the needs and desires of the communities the police serves. Thus, for example, Jamaican black officers may have limited significance for Nigerian or Haitian black communities (Interview, Vince Bevan, Chief of Police, Ottawa). Another question is whether the police should assign recruits to their "own" communities. Considerations include the ability of officers to have authority within their own communities, the ability of the police to match officers to communities, the desire of the officers themselves and the general assessment of the benefits of such matches in bringing police services closer to the community (Interview, Peter Yuen, Staff Sergeant, Toronto Police Service). Indeed, for many of the minority communities, it is argued, it is important to know that the police force is diverse and not necessarily be policed "by their own." From the officer's point of view, they are often uninterested in being assigned to their "own" communities, especially when such assignments limit their promotion opportunities. Promotion is also a major issue for minority communities. "They say the high command is white; there is some assumption that they cannot get to the top; we have to tell them this is a gradual process. . . . I tell them, in ten years you come talk to me. You will see a black deputy or a black chief of police." (Interview, Yuen)

Recruitment of minorities to the police force might help solve issues of under-policing in which communities are alienated from the police, culturally or linguistically. Diversification, in itself however, might have a limited impact. Minority police officers can adopt an attitude that complies with existing police culture in order to succeed in the job and detach themselves from the community in favour of "professionalism." The success of recruitment, therefore, depends on the way the police treat wider questions of diversity. When recruitment is done only for the sake of appearance and recruits have to adjust to existing police culture, argue civic activists, they will do little service to their communities (interview, Yep and Hunter). Police officers themselves recognize the limits of recruitment. "We hire blacks and aboriginals and take pride in that. But after that? A black or aboriginal officer can be a bully and discriminate just like whites" (Interview, Closs).

The training of police officers is central for the ability to attract a diversity of recruits and to operate successfully among minorities. Consequently, training must change prejudices and equip the police with relevant and applicable tools for the operational experience it faces. During the training process, officers have to examine their own assumptions and perceptions about ethnic communities and have the opportunity for direct and positive engagements with communities with whom they may not have had previous contact (Casey, 2000). The RCMP developed a model of training that includes the understanding of clients and their needs, the acquisition and analysis of information, the establishment and maintenance of partnerships for problem solving, the application of response strategies to solve problems, and the assessment and review of the outcomes of actions taken to support continuous improvement (Loree, 2001). In the Ontario Police College, civilian instructors are brought in to teach race relations and introduce diversity questions. Cultural sensitivity is inserted into different parts of the program with the aim of challenging and changing existing biased perceptions and teaching the recruits ways to engage with the communities and work together with them (Interview, Snoddy).

However, training is limited by budgetary concerns and in its impact on officer conduct afterwards. "It is all about budgets," explained one officer. "You have to equip them, which is more expensive these days, train them to use fire arms, situation diffusion and response, and then, if you have money left, cultural sensitivity." Training is ultimately tested in everyday engagement with citizens where it does not always have sufficient influence. "Police officers believe they are good people, and they are . . . some are offended when you talk to them about treating people better. We are talking about diversity, multiculturalism and sensitivity for 20 years but black people and others still feel the same [towards the police]. Why is this so? Some of them are playing it for what it's worth but it is also because we are not focusing upon ourselves as police officers and not paying attention to what we are doing on the streets to some of these people" (Interview, Closs). Therefore, while training, like recruitment, is significant, police attitudes are tested in actual engagements with individuals and communities and are determined by institutional changes in the modes of operation.

Reforming Practices—The Means of Engagement

Over-policing is rooted in biases against minorities that translate into discriminatory practices and mistreatment. Institutional reform, consequently, entails the eradication of police racism and the fair and equal treatment of individuals regardless of race and ethnicity. Racial profiling, the targeting of persons or groups by the police on suspicion of criminal activity based primarily on race, ethnicity or other identifiable marks (www.crr.ca), is an example of discriminatory practices because stereotypes rather than reasonable suspicion single out an individual for different treatment by police officers (Closs and McKenna, 2006). Research in Canada reveals that such stereotypes affect how the police view minorities and, as a result, how minorities view the police.

Already in 1989 a task force report in Ontario concluded that visible minorities believe they are policed differently and treated unfairly by the police (OHRC, p.13). The accusations of unfair treatment of visible minorities turned into a large public controversy when in 2002 the *Toronto Star* newspaper published a series of articles that demonstrated that the Toronto police engage in racial profiling. The Toronto Police Service commissioned an independent review of the *Star*'s analysis that concluded that the *Star* analysis was "junk science" and the conclusions of the articles "completely unjustified, irresponsible and bogus slurs" (Melchers, 2006). Other studies also demonstrated that black people are stopped more often by the police than white people and that good behaviour does not shelter blacks from unwanted police attention. This attention, in turn, serves to further alienate black people from mainstream Canadian society and the police (Wortley and Tanner, 2004). A study conducted by the Kingston Police has found that black young people are more likely to be stopped than white people, but not for different reasons and are slightly more likely to be arrested or charged during police stops (Closs and McKenna, 2006). Police officers, argues Closs, have the opportunity to apply their personal beliefs and values through the discretion used in police stops, checks, warning and charges. Only through monitoring, measuring and knowing how police exercise their power can the police prevent racial profiling (Interview).

While the existence of racial profiling was difficult to prove, as critics of the Star report argued, and the concept itself is an "unfalsifiable claim" (Melchers, 2006), the large controversy forced the police to address the accusations as "the issue of racial profiling has become a significant threat to the ability of police to maintain order, ensure public safety, and prosecute those accused of criminal offences" (Melchers, 2003). Indeed, Aboriginal people and visible minorities were found generally satisfied with the job performed by their local police, but were more critical than the non-Aboriginal/non-visible minority population (Statistics Canada, 2005: 92) and the number of visible minorities who felt that they had been discriminated against or treated unfairly by the police and courts was double (17% versus 8%) that of non-visible minorities (*Ibid*., p.94).

Implementation of programs designed to increase the trust of minorities in the police can reveal a gap between the commitment of senior police officers to multiculturalism and the actual performance of police officers in the street. This gap has been raised by several community activists, who have noted the "intellectual commitment" of senior officers as opposed to the apathy or resistance of lower ranking police officers. Senior police officers believe that the message is filtering down and making a difference in police operations. Even if the senior command is quicker to response to social and political changes, the policies designed, they argue, are gradually being implemented. Moreover, according to police commanders (and even some community activists), the younger generation of police officers, more educated and accustomed to multicultural settings, is more receptive to the changes than the older generation that at times resists the changes.

Implementation also depends on the ability of the police to hold officers accountable for misbehaviour. The police, argue social activists, tend to close ranks and prevent investigations of and actions against fellow officers. Especially important, according to these charges, are the police unions that shield officers charged of abuse (Interview, Yep and Hunter). This claim is rejected by police officers who argue that professional standards are upheld and that improper behaviour is punished, even if, as some officials admit, this is a long and complex process. Kingston's Police Chief Closs agrees that change has to happen "on the streets" and the police have to commit fully to making this change. "They don't want to change the real relations and they are taking the easy way and not having an impact on what is happening on the streets and that is where it has to change or nothing will change" (Interview).

In order to examine whether multicultural policing reforms—recruitment, training and community engagement—are implemented and effective, police practices have to be monitored, the number of complaints and the way they are handled have to be examined, and the level of public satisfaction has to be measured. The number of complaints is another measure of satisfaction but a reduction in the number of complaints can be relevant to one community but not to another and may also be a result of citizens' mistrust of the system. Accordingly, not only the number of complaints is important but also their "origin" and, more importantly, the way they were handled. Complaints that are not handled and officers who are not held accountable can, for all the wrong reasons, contribute to the decline in the number of complaints. Finally, surveys are an important measure of the success of police reforms. Such surveys should be designed to reflect not only overall satisfaction but also the perceptions of different communities and their expectations from the police.

Involvement and Oversight

Expectations of the police from minority communities can be influential, too, during the process of policy making when they can provide their input. Community policing is a form of interaction that involves five main principles. *Partnership perspective* redefines the interaction between the police and the public through a consultative dialogue and interdependence. *Preventive/ Proactive policing* attempts to deal with problems before they arise by cooperation with the community and engagement with the underlying causes of problems rather than their symptoms. *Empowerment* means a decentralization process that is likely to enhance community access to police service and, consequently, its influence over policing. Finally, *cultural sensitivity* compels the police to be attentive to the specific needs of communities.

The Toronto Police system of "community consultative process" shares the responsibility for safety and security with communities, including disadvantaged ones. As it relies on community cooperation, it has to take into account the community's history, culture, existing networks and politics and has to identify the community's assets. "Given the cosmopolitan nature of Toronto's communities, respect for community diversity can be challenging but absolutely necessary" (internal document, Toronto Police). In practice, this involves the assignment of community policing ("neighbourhood") officers who are trained for the role. Officers learn about the community by engaging with it and are able to solve problems (Interview, Yuen). Similarly, in Ottawa, community policing philosophy has been defined in the following manner: "to move in the direction of implementing a problem-oriented policing organization . . . to include the community as an active partner in problem-solving" (www.ottawa police. ca). The involvement of the community includes not only various opportunities for dialogue with and access by the community to the police but also the partnering of police officers with members of the community for critical incidence teams trained to resolve situations between the police and the community. This access has also improved the recruitment from communities that previously stayed away from the police. Finally, this engagement has also provided police with critical information about how to approach and serve communities. "We will not assume to know what is good for the community. This is the first parameter we set. We told the community: you tell us what we need to do in order to serve you better" (Interview, Bevan).

The power de-centralization in community policing raises the question of jurisdiction, especially when the community is a national minority. With aboriginal communities in Canada, for example, reliance on community resources and traditional systems is suggested because the conventional methods of the justice systems fail to deter crime (Interview, David F. Sunhahra, Canadian Police College). Thus, rather than rely solely on the formal justice system, other practices such as community forums and mediation can be useful (Loree, 2000). Aboriginal communities can choose between creating their own independent police force (self-administered policing) and sub-contracting the RCMP to perform police services. The competition seems to encourage the RCMP to develop police programs that appeal to the communities. Indeed, in its brochure the RCMP promises "to assist in the identification and implementation of community policing initiatives . . . through a community consultative group."

Engagement between communities and the police also includes the ability of the community to oversee police policies, procedures and practices. Thus, advisory boards and consultative committees give citizens the opportunities to raise concerns and complaints. In Toronto, Community Police Liaison Committees (CPLC) made up of community volunteers and police service representatives work together to enhance trust and develop solutions for emerging problems within the communities, ethnic or otherwise. The Police Services Board also formed consultative groups that advise the police at different levels including the chief of police, and help make the voices of the community heard. Meetings of the Police Board are open to all members of the public—individuals and groups. In the Toronto case, for example, this civilian oversight committee formulates policies and receives annual reports from the Police Chief on topics such as the effectiveness and implementation of policies related to diversity and multiculturalism.

Conclusions

The findings of this research on police reforms apply also to other public institutions that face contemporary multicultural challenges and have to adapt their services to diverse constituencies. These adaptations, in general, include recruitment patterns, procedures and practices and the input of minority groups on policy-making and implementation. Specifically, over-policing and under-policing are central concerns for minorities that are discriminated against by police procedures. The Canadian context in which civic organizations began to take an interest in the question of policing and, more importantly, various police-initiated reforms, provides an ideal setting to examine these issues.

Changing discriminatory police practices that stem from over-policing and under-policing requires, first and foremost, attention to the problems, needs and desires of minority groups to devise a comprehensive, institutional reform. This study of the Canadian experience identified three central and interrelated issues. First, changes must be made in recruitment patterns that will diversify the police force, allow minority groups hitherto excluded to be part of police services, and narrow the distance between the police and minority communities. Second, changes in attitudes and practices through training programs and a revision of discriminatory practices must occur. And, third, minority groups must have a voice in policy making and oversight of police work to increase legitimacy and confidence. Under-policing and over-policing are often the results of stereotypes and biases that become self-fulfilling prophecies, leading to mutual distrust between the police and minorities. Combined, these interrelated measures suggest a way to narrow the gap between the police and minorities. Their actual impact requires further study.

Bibliography

Barlow, D. and Barlow M. (2000). *Police in a Multicultural Society*. Illinois: Waveland Press.

Brunson, R. and J. Miller. (2006). "Gender, Race and Urban Policing: The Experience of African American Youths" *Gender and Society*, 20, 4 (August), pp. 531-52.

Casey, John. (2000). "International Experiences in Policing Multicultural Societies," *International Journal of Police Science and Management*, 3, 2, pp. 165-77.

Chan, J.B. (1997). *Changing Police Culture: Policing in a Multicultural Society* Cambridge: Cambridge University Press.

Closs, William J. and Paul F. McKenna. (2006). "Profiling a problem in Canadian police leadership: the Kingston Police data collection project." *Canadian Public Administration*, Vol. 49, No. 2 (Summer 2006), pp. 143-60.

Commission on Systemic Racism in the Ontario Criminal Justice System. (1995). *Report of the Commission on Systemic Racism in the Ontario Criminal Justice System: A Community Survey*. Toronto: Government of Ontario.

Desroches, F.J. (1992). "The Occupational Subculture of the Police" in B.K. Cyderman, C.N. O'toole and A. Fleras, ed. *Police, Race and Ethnicity: A Guide for Police Services*. Toronto: Buttersworths.

Erez, E., J. Finckenauer and P.R. Ibarra. (2003). "Introduction: Policing a Multicultural Society," *Police and Society* 7, pp.5-12

Findlay, M. (2004). *Introducing Policing, Challenges for Police and Australian Communities*. Oxford: Oxford University Press.

Fleras, A. (1992). "Police, Race Relations and Ethnicity," B.K. Cyderman, C.N. O'toole and A. Fleras, ed. *Police, Race and Ethnicity: A Guide for Police Services*. Toronto: Buttersworths.

Ghanem, A. (2000) "The Palestinian Minority in Israel: The 'Challenge' of the Jewish State and its Implications," *Third World Quarterly*, 21, 1, pp. 87-104.

Herbert, S. (2006). "Policing the Contemporary City" in V.E. Kappeler, ed., *The Police and Society* Illinois: Waveland Press.

Howell, S.E., H.L. Perry and M. Vile. (2004). "Black Cities/ White Cities: Evaluating the Police," *Political Behaviour* 26, 1.

Inglis, C. (1996). "Multiculturalism: New Policy Responses to Diversity" *MOST Policy Papers*, 4.

Kymlicka, W. (1998). *Finding Our Way*. Oxford: Oxford University Press.

Kelling, G.L. and M.H. Moore. (2006). "The Evolving Strategy of Policing" in Kappeler, *The Police and Society*.

Lithopooulos, L. and G. Rigakos. (2005). "Neo-Liberalism, Community and Police Regionalization in Canada," *Policing: An International Journal of Police Strategies and Management*, Vol. 28, No. 2, pp. 337-52.

Loree, D. (2000). "Policing Across the Cultures: Population Migration and Indigenous Peoples," 1st Sub-Saharan Executive Policing Conference, Durban, South Africa.

_____. (2001). "Police Role and Relationships in Minority Communities: Some Canadian Issues," Sixth International Metropolis Conference, Rotterdam, 2001

Manning, P.K. (2006). "The Police: Mandate, Strategies and Appearances" in Kappeler, *The Police and Society*.

Melchers, R. (2003). "Do Toronto Police Engage in Racial Profiling?" *Canadian Journal of Criminology and Criminal Justice*, 45: 3

_____. (2006). *Before the Law: The Canadian Experience of "Racial Profiling"* RCMP: Research and Evaluation, available online: http://www.rcmp-grc.gc.ca/ccaps/research_eval_e.htm

Murphy, C. (2005). "The Rationalization of Canadian Policing: A Study of the Impact and Implications of Resource Limits and Market Strategies," *The Canadian Review of Policing Research*, (2005) ISSN: 1710-6915.

Ontario Human Rights Commission. (2004). *Paying the Price* http://www.ohrc.on.ca/english/consultations/racial-profiling-report. pdf

Patten Report. (1999). "A new beginning: policing in Northern Ireland," Belfast.

Peled, Y. (1998). "Towards a redefinition of Jewish nationalism in Israel? The enigma of Shas," *Ethnic and Racial Studies*, Vol. 21, No. 4, 1998.

Race Relations and Policing Task Force. (1989). *Report of Task Force on Race Relations and Policing*. Toronto: Queen's Printer for Ontario.

Rouhana, N. (1998). "Israel and its Arab citizens: predicaments in the relationship between ethnic states and ethnonational minorities" *Third World Quarterly*, 19, 2 pp. 277-96.

Smooha, S. (1992). *Arabs and Jews in Israel*. Vol. 2, Boulder and London: Westview Press.

Statistics Canada. (2005). *Criminal Justice Indicators*. Catalogue no. 85-227-XIE

Stenning P.C. (2003). "Policing the Cultural Kaleidoscope: Recent Canadian Experience" *Police and Society* 7, 3, pp. 13-47.

Troper, H. and M. Weinfeld. (1999). "Diversity in Canada" in Troper and Weinfeld, ed., *Ethnicity, Politics and Public Policy*. Toronto: Toronto University Press.

Ungerleider, C.S. (1994). Police, Race and Community Conflict in British Columbia. *Canadian Ethnic Studies*, XXVI (3), 91-104.

Walker, S., C. Spohn and M. DeLone. (2000). *The Colour of Justice: Race, Ethnicity and Crime in America*. Belmont, CA: Wadsworth.

Williams, H. and P.V. Murphy. (2006). "The Evolving Strategy of Police, a Minority View" in Kappeler, *The Police and Society*.

Wortley, S. (2003). "Civilian Governance and Policing in a Multicultural Society: A Discussion Paper," National Forum on Policing in a Multicultural Society, Department of Canadian Heritage, http://www.canadianheritage.gc.ca/progs/multi/pubs/police/civil_e.cfm (downloaded, July 2007)

Wortley, S. and J. Tanner. (2004). "Data, Denials and Confusion: The Racial Profiling Debate in Toronto" *The Canadian Review of Policing Research*, Vol. 1.

Interviews

Bill Beahen, LEAD

Vince Bevan, Chief of Police, Ottawa

William Closs, Chief of Police, Kingston

Sylvio Gravel, Staff Sergeant, Ottawa Police Service

Geoff Grusson, Police Sector Council

David Hallman, Aboriginal Policing Directorate

Wayne Hanniman, National Security Community, Outreach Director, RCMP

Patrick G. Hunter, Canadian Race Relations Foundation

Donald J. Loree, Research and Evaluation, RCMP
Fraser Macaulay, RCMP
Alok Mukherjee, Chair, Toronto Police Service Board
Roger St. Martin, National Community Policing, RCMP
David Snoddy, Ministry of Community Safety and Correctional Services, Ontario Police College
David F. Sunhahra, Canadian Police College
Sandy Yep, Canadian Race Relations Foundation
Peter Yuen, Staff Sergeant, Toronto Police Service

NOTE

1. This research was conducted with the support of the *Israel Association for Canadian Studies* and a visiting position offered me at the *Institute of Canadian Studies* at the University of Ottawa. Special thanks to Dr. Bill Beahen from LEAD, John Herberman from the Police Support Service Branch and to all the interviewees (listed at the end of the article) for being generous with their time and sharing their experience and thoughts with me.

Paper presented at the 12th Biennial Conference of the Israel Association for Canadian Studies, Jerusalem, 2008.

Consumption, Commodification and Choice in Writing by Lillian Ng and Evelyn Lau

ROBYN MORRIS
University of Wollongong, Australia

Cross-Continental Resurrections: The Ghost of Suzie Wong

Gendered and racialised "Orientalised beauties" such as the self-sacrificing geisha Madam Butterfly, or the alluring bar prostitute Suzie Wong, have been referred to as "dangerous" and as "spectres" for women of Asian descent by Asian Canadian critic and writer Larissa Lai (1999 153). The process of equating "the Orient" with the exotic, with Asian, with cheongsam-clad females, is embedded and normalised within the cultural archives of Western art, literature, photography, film and also, in contemporary mass media. This paper explores whether the fiction produced by Lillian Ng from Australia and Evelyn Lau from Canada offers a resistant textuality to such representations of otherness, or whether these writers resurrect Orientalist stereotypes.

The issue of whether the image of the ghost of Suzie Wong hovers in the margins of these writers' texts warrants investigation. More so, the act of constructing positive or negative/ stereotypical representations of "otherness" has resulted in academics being divided in their reaction to both Ng and Lau's literary output. While Lau, from the outset of her literary career has refused to be pigeon-holed as either a Chinese Canadian writer, a feminist or social activist, Ng describes herself as "a Chinese living in Australia" and as an "alien" (Yu 2001 115). Ng also notes that her readership, the people who buy her books, "really have to like Chinese culture and tradition" (Yu 114). This is a loaded statement meaning one of the two things. Firstly, that her books could appeal to a Chinese diasporic community who will understand the colloquialisms of her Chinese characters. On the other hand Ng's books could also be targeted towards a voyeuristic white culture. This culture is characterised by a one-sided consumption and a key methodology in determining the extent of critical ironising evoked by either Ng or Lau's texts is to evaluate their literary production through the notion of consumption, commodification and choice; practices which are intrinsically tied to the thematic of looking relations.

Swallowing Clouds reiterates the link between looking, consumption and choice through the detailed description of the sexual experiences of a young Chinese girl called Syn. Syn is stranded in Sydney after the Tiananmen massacre and, without family or welfare support, finds employment with a Chinese Australian butcher Zhu, eventually becoming his mistress. The blurb on the front cover describing the novel as "an elegant and erotic tale of a most unusual love affair" buys into Orientalised tropes of Asian otherness, and the further description on the back cover of *Swallowing Clouds* as, "Seductive and poignant, rich with Oriental tales and superstitions," indicates that this is a novel that has perhaps been geared towards a predominantly white readership.

In Tseen Khoo's words, "the novel's showcasing of Asian 'sexotica' is intended for a non-Asian readership" (2000 171). The other side to this is the implication that women readers of Asian descent participate in a process in which they appear to be "'perving' on themselves" (Khoo 2000 172). Premised on a stereotypical reconstruction, the image that is being "perved" at is negative and one-dimensional. Khoo critiques the way stereotypes of Asian femaleness as servile, submissive and sexually insatiable are resurrected within Ng's novel, noting:

> *Swallowing Clouds'* complicity with mainstream literary discourse about Asian women and popular promotional strategies exposes the precarious nature of marketing Asian-Australian literature. This

> is especially the case for Asian women's literature, where the predominance of heavily publicized autobiographies and confessionals encourages few deviations in reading perspectives across the entire range of Asian women's writing. (Khoo 2000 166)

When Ng states that "There's a lot of talent among the Chinese writers, but they do not get much recognition by the media" (Yu 121), one wonders if her tale of Oriental(ised) sex under the Australian sun purposefully buys into a white fantasy mechanism.

Ng's depiction of Syn in *Swallowing Clouds* is in danger of a falling prey to a form of neo-Orientalism, one that reifies woman's positioning as object of the gaze. The novel does this through the way Syn is characterised as being acted upon or consumed. Syn has few choices. She takes on employment with Zhu because she regards herself as an illegal immigrant. Zhu takes advantage of her naivety, quickly orchestrating opportunities for him to initiate an affair with her. Syn describes her sex role with Zhu as "the passive one, for she was to portray the garden where 'her flowers bloomed with a hundred scents', to be his Shangrila, his Paradise" (*SC* 56).

This notion of Syn's complete powerlessness and a lack of autonomy are further cemented in the novel when Zhu moves Syn to a house that isolates her from her friends. In a language that fully invokes the world of the harem as it has been imagined by Western eyes, Ng writes: "He kept her in the semi, wrapped up as the Cantonese referred to a kept mistress. She was solely meant for his eyes and his service" (*SC* 140). From cover to cover, *Swallowing Clouds* conforms to a systemised visualising strategy that commodifies Asian female corporeality as exotic and sexualised but also as passive.

This criticism of an authorial reconstruction of gendered passivity has also been levelled at Canadian writer Evelyn Lau's cast of female characters who, like Syn, are similarly situated as passive observers of their sexual entanglements and fixations. Evelyn Lau is a second generation Chinese Canadian who ran away from her parents at fourteen. She survived for two years on the streets of Vancouver. Lau recorded this period of her life in a journal that was later edited and subsequently published under the title, *Runaway: Diary of a Street Kid* (1995). It is an unflinching account of her two years as a drug addict and prostitute and this "peephole" into otherness, along with the novel's commercial success, has accorded her a measure of notoriety while making her a figure of academic and public debate.

Despite name changes, Lau's characters are recycled in her stories as either escorts, prostitutes or mistresses and the majority are, as Rita Wong terms it, fixated with "Old White Daddies" (2001 123). Lau's characters can be read as one-dimensional in that their social, cultural or racial backgrounds are elided, their physical features are not described and as readers, we only observe these women as they dispassionately observe their lives and themselves. These characters are united by their sense of detachment.

In the short story "The Outing" in *Choose Me,* the narrator Julie, who takes on the name Sybil for her visit to a swinger's club, watches as her breasts are being fondled by another man while her client, Hugh watches: "[Sybil] thrust out her chest for him to admire; her body felt numb, and for a moment she imagined she was only a mannequin, made of plaster, with a hollow, airy centre" (*CM* 48). Lau's female characters might observe or gaze upon a culture which otherwise objectifies them but this vision-based interplay is not relational. Lau is in effect, reconstructing Sybil as a patriarchal figure of passivity and it is such constructions or depictions that have academics divided over her work. As Rita Wong notes: "How the women gaze and are gazed upon becomes an entry into reading the volatile power relations under which sex trade workers operate in *Choose Me, Fresh Girls and Other Stories* (2001 125). Lau's positioning of woman as passive does little to challenge existing power relations and as Wong argues, Lau's refusal to enter into a politcised rhetoric "defaults the said writer into reinforcing the conventional political and economic order that masks its reliance on exploitation as 'normal'" (123).

Alternatively, Lily Cho, who reads Lau's work through the rubric of diaspora, argues, "neither obvious as a threat or as an overt retaliation, the gaze of the oppressed subject, of the sex workers, of the racialised women, works through a process of unrelenting objectification" (2007 178). Cho further notes that "Lau's critique of whiteness extends beyond the individual white man in her intimate shredding of middle-class suburban life. She dismantles those hallowed structures of stability, marriage and family" (178). Throughout *Choose Me,* Lau's female characters look back at whiteness and the build-up of their collective observations is vitriolic.

Aging, white males come under unrelenting scrutiny and this perhaps diffuses Rita Wong's claim regarding Lau's obsession with "Old White Daddies." For example, Lau describes the academic Douglas who has "folds in his stomach of incipient fat" (*CM* 25), and Hugh, who "wear[s] a pair of soft dress pants which draped his thick legs loosely, hiding his extra weight, and his white shirt was generously cut, bagging out over the waist [so that he] looked like a stocky wind-up toy, comical, preposterous, a figure of fun" (*CM* 33), or Jeremy, who "seemed terribly old-fashioned in the way he gawked at her nakedness—she believed him when he said he had slept with fewer than a dozen women in his life—and in his clumsy, eager lovemaking, as if he were a boy at the start of his sexual career, rather than a man caught in the physical limitations of its decline" (*CM* 125) or the unnamed sadomasochist in "The Session" who thanks his "Mistress" Mary, for letting him lick her shoes, begging "You'll let me do more won't you? You'll treat me like white trash won't you? You'll spit on me and treat me like garbage?" (*FG* 23)

This scornful gaze back at white patriarchy is quite critical both of the white men who benefit from it and of a social system that others and objectifies the bodies of women. The worrying aspect of this is that Lau's female characters, and this also applies to Syn in Ng's *Swallowing Clouds*, is that they appear to lack a critical self-reflexivity.[1] They do not look into their own constructions of self, or if they do, they find, like Sybil, that there is nothing but passivity, immobility and an airy hollowness. The uneasiness arising from both Ng and Lau's characterisation is their fixation with disempowered females and empowered males. Even the sadomasochist in Lau's short story "The Session," a white man who chooses to play this role, wields economic power in that he is paying the prostitute Mary for her services. Another "escort" is Sybil who in the story "The Outing" significantly notes that she would never have partnered her client to a swingers' night "if Hugh weren't paying her" (*CM* 40). As if to assert his authority, Hugh reminds Sybil: "Remember what we talked about? You know what I want. Don't disappoint me" (*CM* 37). In short, Hugh wants Sybil to have sex with other men and other women while he watches. Hugh's money equates with power over Sybil's body much as Zhu's money and his determination to place Syn as his fully kept mistress does in Ng's *Swallowing Clouds*.

The female characters in Lau's stories appear then, much like Ng's description of Syn, as "trussed-up chickens" (*SC* 82). Both writers offer the (Asian) woman as a delectable, consumable and visually immobile morsel. While the reader of both Ng and Lau's work can be of Asian or Anglo descent, heterosexual or gay, male or female, the questionable "appeal" of their fiction is who this depiction of woman as a spectacle appeals to.

The Commodification of Difference

One way of answering this is to examine the various novel's covers. *Swallowing Cloud's* cover, for example, with a picture of a woman of Asian descent wearing operatic white make-up and "swallowing" a string of black pearls evokes, as Sandra Lyne observes, an image that is consistent with "China doll" stereotypes. Covers matter. As Roy Miki so astutely notes, "the old truism, 'you can't tell a book from its cover', may once have been true, but in this design-obsessed consumerist era, the cover is often a tell-tale sign of power relations, stereotypes, and expectations" (1998 120). The inclusion of the whitened and disembodied face of Evelyn Lau on the back cover of *Choose Me* mirrors the Orientalist stereotyping which characterises the cover of *Swallowing Clouds*.

The titles of Lau's short story collections *Fresh Girls* and *Choose Me* brings to mind the act of judging and consuming flesh but there is another form of consumption happening in the marketing of Lau's work. The blurb on the back cover of *Choose Me* describes the collection as one which "delves into the complexities of human relationships, exploring the ambiguous motives that propel her characters into emotional and sexual entanglements. With prose remarkable for its resonance, its beauty, and its candour, Lau tells the tales of women who long to be chosen by the men they can't have." The front cover of *Choose Me,* with its image of a disembodied female in a tight-fitting satin dress and of *Fresh Girls*, with a woman's naked, opened legs reifies woman as passive, as body and as spectacle.

Rita Wong is highly sceptical of the marketing processes driving Lau's work. Wong observes:

> Before we ever touch the writer's work there is a large machinery that determines who gets published and how they get promoted. Quality of writing is only one factor in this scenario; access to capital, profit margins and preconceptions of what is 'marketable' also play important parts in the process shaping the books to which we as readers have access. [. . .] This commercial machinery makes me suspicious of the ways in which the labour of a writer such as Evelyn Lau gets marketed as an object for consumption. [. . .] Somehow I have the disturbing feeling that, if Lau had not come along, the machine would have found someone else because it needs to have a bit of 'colour' (but not too much) mirroring or serving the symbolic order so that it can disavow its historical and systemic racist tendencies. (2001 123)

While quite often what you see is not what you get and book covers or blurbs can conflict quite markedly with the representation of Asian femaleness inside, for Ng and Lau's fiction this is not strictly true. The covers of Ng and Lau's novels suggest that the ghostly images of Suzie Wong and Madam Butterfly remain a contingent part of the marketing practices of Western publishers. The packaging of fiction by women writers of Asian descent evokes a mirroring, not of the symbolic order, but of Orientalist imagining of Asian femaleness.

The representational politics of Ng's *Swallowing Clouds* is characterised by a neo-orientalism and a lack of critical subtlety. The Prologue to *Swallowing Clouds* contains an explanation of the Buddhist sutra "karma, karma, ohm, ohm" (*SC* xii) which the adulterous woman chants before her drowning. This sets up the tourist-like aspect of the novel. The targeted reader is a sojourner, who, it appears, is going to have, in what was touted in a recent travel advertisement, enticing clients to take "a cheap fling in Asia." *Swallowing Clouds'* lack of self-reflexivity is one of its significant failings. As Khoo writes: "there seems to be a deliberate lack of sophistication in portraying Asianness or gender in *Swallowing Clouds*. Ng's novel is notable not for its specific Australian resonance but, rather, for parading Asian exoticism and ethnic cultural baggage for its audience" (Khoo 2000 172).

Throughout the novel Syn's body is articulated as food and we, as readers, literally ingest her through words. Syn[2] is described as a "plaything, a whore, a delicious side dish, a body" (*SC* 137). Significantly Zhu rarely refers to Syn by her name but by the title "my little dim sum," for she "provided [him] the tangy taste of the wild game bird which his wife of twenty-odd years had failed to supply" (*SC* 136). Furthermore, the title *Swallowing Clouds* instantly brings to mind the act of consumption and of ingestion. "Swallowing clouds" refers to a sex-game initiated by Zhu whereby each partner must ingest the other's partly chewed wontons.

There is an overt woman-as-meat metaphor operating in Ng's *Swallowing Clouds*, one which could have operated as a feminist critique of the representation of the female body in Western film, art, literature and law. The contentious nature of this issue of representation has seen academics divided in their response to the novel.

While Shirley Tucker may argue that "Ng's complex and at times wicked use of Orientalist imagery invokes memories of stereotypes we would rather forget" (2001 130), the novel does far more than simply resurrect such typecasts, it firmly and dangerously embeds them. While Sandra Lyne scathingly describes the novel as a "banal caricature of 'Asian' hyper-sexuality" (8), Kay Schaffer rejects this reading arguing that what Lyne defines as caricature is, in Schaffer's opinion, satire and parody (2003). It is difficult however to find any textual support for Schaffer's less than compelling argument as the novel abounds in passages of neo-orientalist posturing that steers well clear of any rhetorical strategies that could signify social critique.

Shirley Tucker argues that Ng's *Swallowing Clouds* offers a resistance to dominant representations of Asian femininity which have historically swung between notions of her as an exotic lure or as the harbinger of danger or death.[3] Tucker suggests that in *Swallowing Clouds,* "traditional erotic and fearful images of Chinese women are deliberately revived and revised to challenge outdated attitudes that still circulate" (139). When the novel is read however as a palimpsest of filmic and artistic representations of Asian femaleness that is sexually alluring to Western eyes, then Ng's depiction of Syn as a sexually passive "plaything," as a body to be devoured not just by Zhu, but by the voyeuristic gaze of the novel's reader, dangerously buys into the culturally embedded image of an exotic, Asian otherness while also normalising the same heterosexual paradigm of difference.

The novel then, resists critique and emerges as an example of an editing process geared towards marketability. Perpetuation of a representational practice that hyper-feminises and exotifies the Asian female body serves the interest of Western patriarchy, embedding as normal, in cultural and social ideologies, hierarchies of difference that are gender and race based. The recurring image of Syn throughout the novel as a "delicious side dish" clearly indicates that the ghost of Asian, female servility is still hovering. The overarching question that remains is in whose interest does this image serve? The implied observer recording the Orientalist banquet that is *Swallowing Clouds* is not Zhu or the author Lillian Ng, but the Occidental outsider who is, cannibalistically, both the creator (publisher/ marketer) and consumer (reader) of this text.

Lau and the Notion of "Ethical Responsibility"

This is precisely the criticism which has been pointed at Lau's ever-increasing body of fiction. Lau's female characters in her short story collections, *Choose Me* (1999) and *Fresh Girls* (1993) are never described in terms of race and it is difficult in fact, to read race into her short stories. When the twenty-nine year old Melody, who is engaged to marry sixty-five year old Gordon, initially meets his thirty-five year old daughter Janice in *Choose Me*, she is asked: "Will I get a half-brother or—sister? You two would have beautiful children!" (*CM* 102)

This question could imply that Melody's racial ancestry is not the same as that of her intended husband and also, that their potential hybrid offspring would be extraordinary. This passage could also be read as a daughter's sarcastic response to her aging father's liaison with a woman much younger than himself. It is Gordon however who is described in detail. Melody observes him dispassionately: "the mucousy slip of his tongue in her mouth, the oils on his forehead, his ruined and sagging face" (*CM* 107). After five years of marriage, Gordon repulses Melody and yet, as she observes, "the marriage was a mistake she had been eager to make" (*CM* 97). Her union with Gordon "was a final flouting of her critical family and her concerned friends, an act of rebellion. She had displayed him on her arm as a man displays a beautiful woman. Together they commanded the attention she craved, and if there was not envy on their second glances, well, no one knew of their private life together" (*CM* 97). Melody chose to marry Gordon. She also chooses to remain with him. As readers though, we are left to wonder why.

Lau is more subtle than Ng in the way she resists commodification of her work. She achieves this by positioning readers to empathise with characters such as Melody emotionally rather than politically. This same strategy is evoked though some of the female narrators of her short story collection, *Fresh Girls.* The narrator of the first story, titled "Fresh Girls" is a young female sex worker whom an older client calls "Baby Girl." This narrator notes that: "To him, and others, I'm still in my Lolita years, but I have a birthday coming up soon. I'll be twenty, and what then?" (*FG 7).* This girl appears trapped by a sense of hopelessness over her economic situation. She needs the work because she has, "what one could call expenses" (*FG* 11). This comment is worthy of exploration and could be Lau's way of critiquing both the commodification and devaluation of female flesh. As Lau herself found out in her years on the streets of Vancouver, the only commodity, the only way of earning money to pay for her "expenses," was to sell her body.

This line of critique is not pursued however and the narrator notes with a detached apathy: "I never wanted to get older like ordinary teenagers. I knew there was nothing up there to look forward to except smelly old regulars and a parade of new girls, sixteen, seventeen, coming in illegally through the doors of every massage parlour in town and crowding me out" (*FG* 11). Again, this statement could offer some critique of the trade of Asian women's bodies who enter, illegally or otherwise, the white nation, but because of their alien status are tied to working life in which their bodies and their earnings are controlled by others such as Mario, the owner of the massage parlour in "Fresh Girls."

Choice, for the narrator of "Fresh Girls," is linked to the commodification of her flesh and she realises at the close of the story that her value decreases with each passing year. Despite the overall sense of hopelessness, Lau's prose does evoke sympathy for the narrator's plight and while this evocation of sympathy does not equate with explicit criticism of the patriarchal social order which evaluates these girls' value, there is a sense that Lau is standing in the margins of these stories, observing her social world with a critical, ironising and ethically responsible eye. However, the overall response to Ng and Lau's work has been that their fiction mirrors rather than critiques the dominant patriarchal social order. Both writers enter into the thematics of looking relations producing fiction which is in danger of embedding Asian female corporeality as subservient and as an object to be looked upon. This paper's evaluation of Ng and Lau's fiction and the divisive critical responses regarding the ethical responsibility or extent of critical ironising within their work is intended to provide an evaluative platform from which to determine whether the voices emerging from the sites of Asian Australian and Asian Canadian literature diverge or merge.

NOTES

1. This notion of the way women, and especially women of Asian descent, are positioned as object of the gaze—as passive and doll-like—is a dominant motif in the fiction of the Canadian-based writer, Larissa Lai. Lai's work provides a critical comparison to Lau and Ng's through its consistent and strident critique of this historicised subjectification.
2. Tseen Khoo notes that the name is a deliberate play on the homonyms "Syn" and "sin" (2000 166). This offers a double meaning in that Syn's sexual liaison with Zhu in contemporary Australia is "sinful" and also that Syn is now being punished for having been an adulterer in a past life in rural, feudal China. Neither of these possibilities allows for a positive reading of Asian female sexuality.
3. Tucker also acknowledges that *Swallowing Clouds* is part of the tradition of Asian American women's writing. She argues that the novel's narrative of consuming passion is quite literally played out

in this unorthodox 'love story' despite Ng's deliberate interweaving of familiar romantic tropes and a sub-text of female oppression made popular by diasporic Chinese women writers such as Maxine Hong Kingston, Jung Chang, Amy Tan and Adeline Yen Mah (2001 124).

Works Cited

Cho, Lily. "Dislocations and Diaspora: Reading Evelyn Lau's *Choose Me.*" *Studies in Canadian Literature.* 32: 1 (2007): 173-91.

Khoo, Tseen. "Selling Sexotica: Oriental Grunge and Suburbia in Lillian Ng's *Swallowing Clouds.*" *Diaspora: Negotiating Asian-Australia*, ed. Helen Gilbert, Tseen Khoo & Jacqueline Lo. St. Lucia: Univ. of Qld. Press. 2000. 164-72.

Lai, Larissa. "Political Animals and the Body of History." *Canadian Literature.* 163 (Winter 1999): 145-54.

Lau, Evelyn. *Choose Me: Stories.* Toronto: Vintage Canada, 1999.

———. *Fresh Girls and Other Stories.* Toronto: Harper Collins, 1993.

———. *Runaway: Diary of a Street Kid.* Toronto: Coach House, 1989.

Lyne, Sandra. "Consuming Madam Chrysanthème: Łoți's 'doll' to *Shanghai Baby.*" *Intersections.* 8 (October 2002). Cited 25/11/2006 available from wwwsshe.murdoch.edu.au/intersections /issue8/lyne.html

Murdoch, Anna King. "The China Syndrome." *The Age.* Saturday Extra. (21 March, 1998): 8.

Ng, Lillian. *Swallowing Clouds*. Sydney: Penguin, 1997.

————. *Silver Sister.* Melbourne: Mandarin, 1994.

Ommundsen, Wenche. "Birds of Passage? The New Generation of Chinese-Australian Writers." *alter/Asians: Asian-Australian Identities in Art, Media and Popular Culture*, ed. Ien Ang et al, Sydney: Pluto Press, 2000. 89-106.

Schaffer, Kay. "Transforming Trauma: Post Tiananmen Narratives and the Chinese Intellectual Diaspora." *The Regenerative Spirit: Polarities of Home and Away, Encounters and Diasporas, in Post-Colonial Literatures*, ed. N. Bierbaum, S. Harrex & S. Hosking. Adelaide: Lythrum Press 2003. 145-57.

Tucker, Shirley. "Beyond Belief: Representation and Revolt in Lillian Ng's *Swallowing Clouds.*" *Bastard Moon*: *Essays on Chinese-*

Australian Writing, ed. W. Ommundsen. *Overland.* 7 (2001): 125-44.

Wong, Rita. "Market Forces and Powerful Desires: Reading Evelyn Lau's Cultural Labour." *Essays on Canadian Writing*. 73 (Spring 2001): 122-42.

Yu, Ouyang, "An Interview with Lillian Ng." Ed. W. Ommundsen. *Bastard Moon*: *Essays on Chinese-Australian Writing. Overland.* 7 (2001): 111-24.

Rohinton Mistry's *Family Matters*: A Reading about Death

BETH RUSHTON
Res. Sch., Sydney University, Australia

In this paper I will consider how Rohinton Mistry's novel *Family Matters* is a study of death. Death, dying and loss shape the novel, the lives of the characters and their relationships with each other. No fewer than six main characters die during the course of the novel, which gives Mistry plenty of opportunity to meditate on the meaning of this universal theme. After a brief synopsis of the novel I will consider in some detail the deaths within the novel. I will consider how death and dying are introduced and the ways that Mistry ensures a growing emotional reaction to the deaths as the novel progresses. I consider how moral judgments are made on people's actions through the way Mistry constructs their deaths. This paper concludes with a consideration of the parallels between the deaths of individual characters and their literal and symbolic links to the broader theme of the death of tolerance amongst Indian society.

Family Matters is the story of the relationships in the extended family of Nariman Vakeel. Nariman's decline due to terminal illness—Parkinson's disease—frames the story and the novel tracks in detail his penultimate year before death and the epilogue provides a brief view of his death and the family's life following it. When the novel opens, Nariman is living with his two middle-aged step-children Jal and Coomy Contractor, but following a fall that results in a broken leg he is sent to live with his daughter. Roxana lives with her husband Yezad and their two sons, Murad and Jehangir. During the novel Yezad goes from being a man who scoffs religion to being more pious than his wife's half-sister Coomy. Both he and his son Jehangir flirt with corruption and deception. Daisy Aunty, a neighbour at Chateaux Felicity plays her violin for the dying Nariman on a regular basis, as Coomy schemes to ensure that Nariman is unable to return to their flat. The parallel story of Nariman's relationship with the non-Parsi Lucy and the consequent family scandal resulting in his marriage to Yasmin Contractor are remembered in his flashbacks. As these family dramas unfold, so too does political turmoil in Indian society as it becomes increasingly intolerant of diversity. Religious and nationalist violence and fundamentalism are being enforced by the Shiv Sena, resulting in literal and figurative deaths in the novel. At the end of the novel, following Coomy's death, Roxana and her family, including Nariman, all move back in with Jal Contractor.

Death and dying are introduced in the opening pages of the novel as the frail Nariman wakes and goes for a walk. Mistry contrasts the 'stale emptiness of the flat' with the 'bustling life' of the market, and Nariman's frail body with the 'glistening', 'irresistible', 'voluptuous' vegetables that 'blossomed' (5). Nariman never buys anything from the markets and believes that the stall-holders understand why he shops there, to come into contact with full and bustling life. This contrast is a powerful device and the scenes Mistry describes are very evocative, establishing a tension between full and unattainable life and Nariman's expected and impending death. It is not his illness and his dying state that make the flat stale however, but his bitter stepchildren's reaction to it. Coomy Contractor in particular resents being forced to care for Nariman while he is dying.

Death is gently introduced to the reader in *Family Matters*. Given that one of the main protagonists is an elderly man suffering from a terminal illness the reader is primed for death, yet Nariman is actually the last of many characters to die during the course of the novel. As the novel progresses, the characters that die are increasingly well-developed and the deaths happen in a more contemporary time frame, ensuring that the deaths have an increasing impact on the reader. Mistry introduces death slowly and carefully to the story and builds it up into a climax when Nariman finally dies.

The very first death of the novel is that of Jal and Coomy's father Palonji Contractor. However, because it is so early in the novel, the character previously unknown until his death is mentioned and it is told with humour, it has little emotional impact on the reader (8). The first death where the immediate emotional impact is explored also has minimal impact on the reader. Nariman tells Jehangir about the death of his friend's pets sixty-two years ago (164-65). The death lacks immediacy for the reader, as the deaths were of animals not known to us, and they happened a long time past. This emotional distance allows the reader to empathise with Jehangir's strong reaction. This is the first time Jehangir calculates that death is threatening his grandfather's life, due to old age without the complication of a terminal illness considered. As Jehangir realises that 'the arithmetic was threatening' his grandfather's life (166), he becomes very upset, especially as moments earlier he had been 'aching with grief' about the loss of the pets (165). This contrast is a useful device deployed by Mistry to show the large emotional impact that death can have, and it also prepares the reader for how the characters might react to Nariman's death, which we are expecting.

This scene in the novel is also an early example of death unfavourably affecting life. Jehangir retreats to the balcony crying and this prevents him from performing his evening greeting ritual with his father. Yezad becomes annoyed by the way that death is intruding on his life, yet another death later in the course of the novel results in the loss of his job, forcing a far greater intrusion than the mere interruption of his evening ritual. Yezad is in fact the character who changes most during *Family Matters*—as his negative traits are developed under the strain of his family caring for the dying Nariman and the loss of his job due to the death of his boss. His new-found pious nature is scoffed at by his eldest son and also by Mistry, and these internal changes to Yezad's character parallel the broader death of tolerance in society.

Mistry introduces death in a way that builds up the emotional impact of each successive death as the story progresses. Following the humour-told death of Palonji Contractor and the re-told story of long-dead pets, two characters—who are slightly more developed—die, as told in a flashback of Nariman. The deaths of his wife Yasmin and his forbidden and spurned premarital sweetheart Lucy are the first instance where characters that have been developed with some depth die (380). These two women were in a battle for Nariman's love. After a long affair with Lucy, Nariman finally decided to follow his family's wishes and marry a fellow Parsi, the widowed Yasmin Contractor. Yasmin decided to confront Lucy directly following Lucy's persistent stalking of Nariman, and during their conflict the two women fell off a roof and died together. The deaths of Palonji Contractor, the pets, Lucy and Yasmin lack immediacy; they all occurred in the past, before the novel opens. Mistry keeps us emotionally distant from them in the way the deaths are told utilising different devices: humour, flash-backs, an elderly character recalling a childhood memory.

When Coomy and Edul Munshi die, it is the first time that deaths unfold before the reader rather than being remembered by a character or told through a flash-back (395). This gives these deaths a sense of immediacy and brings the reader emotionally closer to them. These characters, particularly Coomy, have been well-developed, again adding to the emotional impact of their deaths. Although they die from an accident, Mistry includes clues as to their impending deaths that the astute reader may pick up on. On page 391 the girder being used in the renovations in the Contractor flat is placed below its 'final resting place', language that is evocative of death. It is at the same location four pages later where Edul Munshi and Coomy die as a result of this girder. Edul is the interfering, bumbling neighbour who fashions himself as a Mr Fix It. Coomy has enlisted his help as she relies on his incompetence as part of her scheme to make the flat uninhabitable for Nariman to return from Roxana's. Her nastiness leads directly to her death as her plan backfires, with Edul's incompetence killing them both. Yezad's boss Mr. Kapur dies on the same day as Coomy and Edul. He is a direct victim of the growing intolerance in the broader political sphere.

Nariman is the final character to die in the novel. His death is very moving and the most memorable death of any novel I have read. He is given a very dignified death, as Daisy Aunty, a violinist with the Bombay Symphony Orchestra, dresses in her fancy performance clothes, arguing that Nariman deserved her in her finery (473). All the family were gathered around Nariman's bed to say goodbye in the evening. The immediacy of the death again increases, for several reasons. Nariman is the character that we as readers have known the longest period of time and we have been expecting his death since very early on in the novel as his frailty was highlighted and his terminal illness divulged in the opening pages. Although Nariman's final hours are told through the epilogue, set four years later, the immediacy is preserved as Jehangir vividly recalls the details of his last day. The narrative voice in the epilogue shifts from a second person, one with shifting perspectives that dominated the rest of the novel, to Jehangir in the first person. While the telling of Nariman's death by the boy who was earlier so deeply affected by the death of pets unknown to him could have made this final death more emotionally confronting, this shift in narrative voice does detract from the novel. It was an unnecessary change in perspective on Mistry's part and its benefits were outweighed by the distraction it caused.

Many characters died throughout the novel, which allows Mistry to make moral judgments about his characters through the nature and construction of their deaths. Mistry implicitly asks whether characters should be forgiven for their misdeeds in life.

Coomy had nastily plotted to get out of her family duties and she died as a direct result of her scheming. In addition, Mistry magnified her crimes by positioning her body close to Edul's, thus fuelling further hatred and suspicion of Coomy by Edul's widow Manizeh. This coupled with Jal telling the rest of the family about Coomy's plotting ensures that Coomy is remembered negatively with her character flaws at the fore. Coomy was not a likeable character—although of course Mistry is never black and white and his characters are far from two-dimensional. It is in particular her lack of commitment to family that appears to be her biggest flaw in the eyes of Mistry.

Whether or not one should be judged in death very much depends on the "crimes" the character has performed in life. Mistry positively judges tolerance and relationships between Parsis and others. Nariman's relationship with the non-Parsi Lucy was ostensibly his greatest crime in life. However, the consequences of conforming to family and societal expectations were the gross unhappiness of all the family members that are made clear through the novel and the deaths of both the women in his life. Mistry further confirms this judgment against intolerance by giving Nariman the most dignified death of the novel, in complete contrast to Coomy's. If the punishment fits the crime, and the death befits the life, then Mistry is stating very strongly that both commitment to family and tolerance are desirable.

The death of tolerance occurs at an individual, family and societal level in *Family Matters*. In broader society, the increasing Shiv Sena violence reflects a conservative nationalist fundamentalism, and Mr Kapur's death is directly linked to this intolerance. At an individual level, Yezad's character changes the most and best reflects this theme, from a tolerant man who mocked religious performance to an incredibly pious one who also believes in Parsi Puritanism. Mistry's descriptions of him are unflattering, and Yezad himself becomes more intolerant as he suffers from guilt about his own dishonesty. Two generations in the family demonstrate intolerance towards relationships with non-Parsis. Nariman's family put extended pressure on him to end his relationship with Lucy, and this same intolerance is now being perpetrated by Yezad against Murad (467). Mistry made Lucy and Yasmin die together as the debate they were embroiled in, about the possibilities or otherwise of relationships between Parsis and others, was unable to be resolved. Now with the possibility of history repeating itself, Mistry is careful to end the novel on a note of cautious hope about this prejudice pervading the Parsi community, as Yezad concedes and allows Murad's non-Parsi girlfriend to attend his birthday dinner, although they do still fiercely argue with each other regularly. This quest for Parsi Puritanism led to many deaths. Jal has a talk with the doctor and policeman following Coomy's death, both of whom are very concerned about the impending death of the Parsi community, caused through inter-marriage (412). Through the unhappiness for all affected by the replacement of a love-match with a non-Parsi to Nariman's marriage to a Parsi, Mistry negatively judges this puritanism and intolerance. This prejudice is portrayed as undesirable throughout the course of *Family Matters*.

Throughout this paper I have examined the ways that Mistry has constructed and made death and dying central in his novel *Family Matters*. As the novel progresses, the deaths have an increased immediacy and the characters are more developed before they die, resulting in an increasing emotional resonance in the reader. Mistry shows how death shapes the lives of the living and dying. He makes moral judgments through the different deaths about their respective character flaws, as well as using it as a narrative device to explore broader issues of tolerance and prejudice in Indian society. Ultimately, he uses death as a central theme to great effect in this novel.

Cultural Ethos and Ethnic Values: A Study of Rohinton Mistry

JAGDISH BATRA
Hindu College, Sonepat, India

"When a culture vanishes, humanity is the loser," comments Inspector Masalawala in Rohinton Mistry's novel *Family Matters*. This concern about a progressive community with a glorious past and a dismal future underlines the writer's overzealous attempt at detailing the lifestyle and culture of the Parsis wherever he finds the opportunity in his fiction. Mistry's characters, quite commonly, represent the Parsi community, whose identity has been historically problematized. It all started with their exodus following Muslim invasion of ancient Persia which led to their settlement in the hospitable environs of Gujarat, though on condition of off-loading marginally their cultural baggage. During the British rule, they hobnobbed with the master race and got alienated from the native people. At this point, the Western lifestyle and mores permeated the Eastern inheritance of the Parsis. Post-independence, they had to adjust with the same people whom a few generations of Parsis had once learnt to deride and despise.

In recent past, another dimension has been added. A large number of young Parsis have chosen to and still continue to migrate to the West, Mistry himself being one of them, hoping to recover a life of comfort and pride. But their Western experience has reminded some of Matthew Arnold's famous lines: "Standing between two worlds, one dead/ The other powerless to be born." Rohinton Mistry's three novels, viz., *Such a Long Jour-*

ney, A Fine Balance and *Family Matters* and a collection of stories *Tales from Firozsha Baag* deal with this mixed bag of experiences, in an idiom that has ensured classic status for his works. In the case of the Indian Parsis, this identity is essentially constituted by their religious and cultural positions and practices. It also depends upon their equation with other categories of people in the society.

Since the question of cultural identity is rooted in history, the historical trajectory needs to be explored in detail here. The Parsis have had a glorious past. Theirs is one of the oldest civilizations on this earth. During those times, the force that bound the people together was located in the faith that they practised. The people of ancient Iran belonged to the Indo-European branch of the Aryans and their history goes as far back as 2000 B.C., when Zarathustra, the Prophet of ancient Iran is believed to have been born. Some of the great figures of the past whose names are etched in the minds of the Parsis are Cyrus the Great and Khushrau I also called Nowshirwan-i-Adil, i.e., Nowshirwan the Just.

In 614 A.D., Khushrau II attacked Jerusalem and captured it, killing 50000 Christians. This resulted in counter-attacks by Christian forces bringing much misery to the people. After the death of Prophet Mohammad, the Arabs started a series of invasions on Iran and were successful in. 641 A.D in capturing it. Their avowed intent was to spread their faith through force. The last king of the Persian empire Yazdegard went into hiding but after ten years he was captured and assassinated by the Muslims. The followers of Zarathustra had to flee, get converted or lie low. How the Parsis take pride in recalling their glorious past is very well shown by the words spoken on the Parsi wedding, in which the day and year is calculated from "Emperor Yazdegard of the Sassanian Dynasty of auspicious Iran . . . in accordance with the rites and rules of the Mazdayasnans" (Nanavutty 24).

The question does torment Mistry: Who is a true Parsi? He does throw up ideal characters. They have Parsi names, they pray and observe rituals the way Parsis are expected to do. Also they eat and dress in a particular way. Not all of them are ideal though. In the *Tales from Firozsha Baag*, we do meet a number of characters who need not be remembered—like Rustomji or Khorshedbai. But there is this lad Percy who grows into a thinking individual and the one who has the courage and vision to put his ideas into action and lead an authentic life. In *Such a Long Journey*, we come across Gustad Noble, who, true to his name, transcends the self and remains unshaken in his essential goodness in the face of countless vicissitudes of life—a son turning hostile, an ailing daughter, the pin-pricks of the neighbours and the unsavoury and overmuch risky adventure foisted upon him by his one-time friend Major Bilimoria. If he is shown praying in the opening scene of the novel, he is no less religious even at the end of the novel. If anything, this religiosity has taken a new meaning, for he prays "as much for Tehmul as for Jimmy. And for Dinshawji, for Pappa and Mamma, for Grandpa and Grandma, all who had had to wait for so long" (*SALJ* 337) In the end he is shown tearing the black paper off the windowpanes in a symbolic move to let into his home the light from 'outside.' There is no need for fear thereafter! That is his net gain even though poetic justice has resolved all his problems. He has realized himself and attained a kind of salvation through identifying the self with the society.

Dina Dalal in *A Fine Balance* presents the picture of a fighting female who has been wronged by destiny in the form of premature death of her loving husband. But beyond that her own brother is bent upon killing her through kindness. Dina struggles to stand on her own feet but cannot and has to come back to the condescending fold of her big brother whose wife, more than her brother Nusswan, sees to it that her position is no better than that of a domestic help. She is not the god-fearing type like Gustad but she is, nevertheless, a true Parsi who with the passing of time, transcends the worldly barriers of race, caste and creed and feels one with the tailor-turned-beggar duo Ishvar and Omprakash.

Yezad, in *Family Matters*, is not such a one who could take his place with the sublime figures talked about in the preceding paragraphs. He has yielded to the temptation and taken the devil's path. And though he realizes his mistake after it is too late, poetic justice lands him in a limbo where even constant praying does not bring peace of mind, either to him or to his near and dear ones. Jehangir notes,

> My father has emerged from the bathroom, and is doing his kusti by the cabinet. His expression is always very intense when he prays. He finishes tying the knots and sits with his prayer book before the electric afargaan, in the wooden chair no one else is allowed to use. He sits as though he is carrying a secret burden, whose weight is crushing him. He frowns a lot, his face contorting in pain. He doesn't just close his eyes, he clenches the eyelids shut, the cheeks rising, the brows pressing downwards to squeeze out whatever it is that haunts him. His Avesta recitations—the various Yashts, Gehs, Nyaishes, depending on the hour—are like a rebuttal, a protest. He is locked in a struggle. (*FM* 465)

Prayers do not reveal to him the truth that lies beyond rituals in a changed heart that does not discriminate against his son's girlfriend on the basis of her non-Parsi identity. The reaction from his son is not totally unwarranted when he fails to find the father that Yezad used to be. Perhaps Mistry wanted the Hindu businessman Kapoor, Yezad's employer, to be the ideal character. He is truly a cosmopolitan figure and in picking him, Mistry too has transcended his restricted choice of characters, for goodness knows no such bounds.

An individual could be sincere towards himself, he could hear and be answerable to his own inner voice and that would be the true authentic identity, but in the human society in which we live, the identity is known by the markers decided upon by society, for it is a mark of social recognition and import and plays a vital role in social interaction and commerce. This identity carries the burden of history and is transmuted into categories like race, creed, colour, nationality etc. There are also the markers of age, sex, vocation that are of import in day-to-day transaction of work. But when we talk about the identity, we mean by and large, the earlier set of categories. In this, as suggested, past becomes more important than even the present.

Mistry's reference to the Parsis' past is not in jingoistic terms; it is a muted one, as in the story 'Swimming Lessons' in *Tales from Firozsha Baag,* in the form of the reaction of Kersi's father to his son's stories. He recounts the great figures of ancient and modern history and wishes that his son would write "something positive about Parsis." (245) More than that, Mistry's novels as also his stories are full of references to religious aspect of the Parsi life. The opening scene in *Such a Long Journey* begins with the chief character Gustad Noble offering morning prayers to the tying and untying of *kusti.* In *Family Matters*, the procedure for normal daily fire worship in an *agiary* is mentioned in detail. Again, the celebration of the *Behram roje*, the Parsi new year is the theme of the story 'One Sunday' in *Tales from the Firozsha Baag*. While *A Fine Balance* carries brief description of Dina's wedding, the detailed narration of death rituals occurs almost in each one of these works.

During the British rule in India, the western influence cast its shadow on the Parsis, who, as businessmen, felt obliged to befriend the rulers. The proximity also spilled over to the political field. Some prominent Parsi merchants helped the British rulers but the British merely used them. Apart from the British, there were also the French and the Portuguese, ruling the coastal areas. The Parsi entrepreneurs often acted as mediators between different parties. This also helped the Parsis in securing government jobs. The Christian missionaries were greatly facilitated in their work by the ruling class at that time. With the rise of the national sentiment in India, the Hindus preferred not sending their children to educational institutions run by the Christian missionaries but the Parsis did not have any such scruples with the result that their children became more proficient in English than others. The continued proximity of the Parsis to the Englishmen also created a chasm between the Parsis and other communities in India despite significant contribution made to the freedom struggle by certain towering Parsi figures like Ferozeshah Mehta, Dadabhai Naoroji, Dinshaw Wacha, Bhikaji Cama *et al.* The Parsis still continue to contribute to the national life in an impressive manner even though they comprise only 0.016% of the total population of India. Take any area—business, politics, social service, administration, professionals, armed forces, sports, science, arts, music, literature, journalism—you surely find the Parsis there.

The westernized lifestyle of the Parsis is a fact reflected in his works by Mistry also. Whether it is the surfeit of English rhymes and song-lines in *Such a Long Journey*, the birthday celebrations in *pucca* English style in *Family Matters*; the handling of love-sick Lucy by a married Professor or the way of addressing his father-in-law as 'chief' by Yezad in *Family Matters*, English culture seems to have permeated the Parsi lifestyle to a great extent. Alcohol consumption is common not only among menfolk but also among women and young boys. Thus, on the occasion of Roshan's birthday, Dilnavaz takes a few sips from her son Darius's beer glass (*SALJ* 46). The elderly lady Tehmina is hooked on to her evening scotch and soda and the Boyce family keeps its weekly supply of beef in Najamai's refrigerator (*TFFB* 26). All this shows the Parsis living in a world that is different from the common Indian way of life. Whereas this has affected their estimation in the eyes of ordinary Indians, the politico-religious turmoil in the wake of Babri demolition episode has unnerved many Parsis also. Nilufer Bharucha aptly remarks: "In decolonized India, the exalted position enjoyed by the Parsis during the Raj has been eroded and increasing dominance by the majority Hindu community has marginalized them. Parsis today are trying to reorient themselves to this new much reduced role." (Bharucha 42) To this unenviable new role can be added some other problems impinging upon their cultural identity.

The Parsis left the shores of ancient Persia for the sake of religion and have maintained their separate identity on that basis.

But the modern Parsi youth, a product of western education and upbringing, is distancing himself from religion. Perhaps for this reason, Mistry has portrayed in his novels a fallen world where prayers do not usher in an equitable and humane society. The youth is particularly disenchanted as is the case with the Parsi youth Maneck Kohlah, who, in utter desperation, calls God 'the Bloody Fool' and questions his judgement of fair and foul which, according to him, is as simple as reading a balance sheet. Says Maneck, "He would have been sacked long ago if He were managing a corporation" (*AFB* 585). The child Jehangir asks in his innocence: "If only Dada Ormuzd could help me understand! Why must prayer and religion lead to so many fights between father and son? Is that His will?" (*FM* 466). Who would give answers to such questions? The education in the Parsi religion is not organized well. At best, they have semi-literate *dustoors* or priests. There is no facility like the Sunday church school or a visiting pastor. Religious debates are unheard of. This leaves a lot to be desired from the point of view of the young generation.

Population is an important factor in the visibility and viability of any ethnic identity. Over the years, there has been a drastic fall in the population of the Parsis. The total population of the Parsis in India stood at one lakh in 1961, 90,000 in 1971 census, 75-80,000 in 1987 census (Haldar 102) and is estimated to be around 60,000 at present. Mistry is, in fact, concerned about this alarming decline in the population and is said to have stated in an interview: "when the Parsis have disappeared from the face of the earth, his writing will 'preserve a record of how they lived'" (Bharucha 45). In *Family Matters*, Dr. Fitter and Mr. Masalawala have a lively discussion on the issue of depleting numbers with the latter holding the opinion that in fifty years, there would be no Parsis left, and the former responding with a comic flair that their remains would be christened after the dinosaurs:

> "You [Jal] will be named Jalosauras," said Dr. Fitter. "I will be Shapurjisauras. If they find my father's bones, we will have a Pe-

> stonjisauras with a pugree on his head. And our inspector here, who loves his Scotch, will be the powerful
>
> "Whiskysauras, a magnum of Blue Label tucked under his arm." (*FM* 412)

Masalawala holds the 'poison' of individualism responsible for this dismal state and offers certain mock-serious solutions that fit in well with the small talk at the liquor table whereby Mistry suggests that even those who are serious about the issue are discouraged due to the lukewarm response from others in the community. Quite a few like Jal find solace in nephews and nieces rather than sons and daughters. (*FM* 417)

In fact, in an age of cut-throat competition, economic prosperity takes precedence over family. Late marriages hamper chances of sound growth. Jal and Coomy, the siblings in *Family Matters,* have not married even though they are well past their marriageable age. In this, what comes as an eye-opener is the fact that the lack of adequate housing facility in Parsi buildings and high rentals elsewhere in Bombay has also played their part (*FM* 413). Apart from it, the persona in the story 'Swimming Lessons' refers to two major problems haunting the Parsis: "We are the chosen people where osteoporosis is concerned. And divorce. The Parsi community has the highest divorce rate in India. It also claims to be the most westernized community in India. Which is the result of the other? Confusion again of cause and effect" (*TFFB* 230). With a high proportion of ageing, ailing Parsi population, the future in terms of numbers seems bleak.

While expecting the world around to change, their own house must be set in order by the Parsis. In the situation in which the community finds itself, organizations claiming to work for the community should have discharged their duties honestly and zealously in safeguarding the cultural identity and in instilling its awareness in the Parsi youth. But clearly, Mistry is not satisfied. Therefore, in his oeuvre, the work of the Parsi Panchayats and Trusts takes a drubbing. Rustomji of 'Auspicious Occasions'

(*TFFB* 5) loses his cool at the very mention of the Parsi trust because it has failed to maintain well the apartment block in which he stays with his wife. One big reason for the failure of the Parsi panchayats is reported to be their hereditary character. That is certainly an anachronism in our times. The Panchayat is doing little to come to terms with the issue of falling population of the Parsis. Besides, promotion of Parsi culture and teaching of Zoroastrianism to the new generation are tasks which have to be undertaken urgently.

While safeguarding its identity, an ethnic community has also to adjust with other communities in society. It is quite normal to see stereotypes at play in this field. While the dominant community is quoted in *Such a Long Journey* as calling Parsis 'crow eaters,' the latter retaliate by referring to their liking for asafetida. Similarly, in *Tales from Firozsha Baag*, the Parsis call the natives 'ghatis' and the maidservants 'Gangas,' the dominant community members call them 'bawaji.'

While these are normal prejudices that plague mankind everywhere, a big factor that presents a hurdle to the Parsis' assimilation in the present Indian society is the Indian brand of politics. Mistry hates the political tomfoolery aimed at grabbing power through vote bank politics, at its best and through hook or crook, at its worst. There is hardly any human consideration in it. This creates aversion and distrust in the minorities. Mistry has castigated the political leadership for the ills that befell the nation in the wake of proclamation of Emergency. How this ill-advised step of the late Prime Minister Indira Gandhi affected the man in the street, has been graphically illustrated in *A Fine Balance*. Prior to it, the Nagarwala scandal during the Bangladesh liberation war proved to be Mrs. Gandhi's Achilles' heel. The plot of *Such a Long Journey* rested on it. In *Family Matters*, Mistry based the central action on the situation arising out of Shiv Sena agitation for the so-called 'sons of the soil' in Bombay. This type of political bungling presents a stumbling block in the way of the Parsis' healthy adjustment in Indian society at a time when other options like migrating to developed countries are available to them.

In these changed times, the youth—Parsis or others—particularly aspire to be world citizens, thanks to their education, skills and expanding world markets. Due to the competition from other communities in India, the Parsis have migrated in large numbers to other countries like Canada, New Zealand, Australia etc. Those who cannot make it to the promised land—Canada, in the case of Yezad in *Family Matters*—retain a life-long scar on their psyche.

Mistry has very vividly captured the mood of the Gen-next in the character of Jamshed in his story 'Lend Me Your Light' (*TFFB*). He just cannot put up with things in Bombay and would be happy to catch the next flight back to New York. It is not necessary that the westward immigration would be successful. Even if we leave out Sarosh's 'eastern bowels, western seat' problem with its fantastic medical solutions on account of high imagination, we cannot dismiss his observation couched in oracular language that could be true of many exiles: "When you shall these unlucky deeds relate, speak of me as I am; nothing extenuate, nor set down aught in malice: tell them that in Toronto once there lived a Parsi boy as best as he could. Set you down this; and say, besides, that for some it was good and for some it was bad, but for me life in the land of milk and honey was just a pain in the posterior." (*TFFB* 168)

The issue of identity confusion is all the more severe in the case of a person living the life of an exile, for it is the case of what Derrida would call 'double displacement.' According to Derrida, "the nation is rooted first of all in the memory or anxiety of a displaced—or displaceable—population. It is not only time that is out of joint, but space, space in time, spacing." (Bharucha 55). The exile is haunted by the nostalgia of his homeland while he is hardly at home in his adopted country.

The other character in the story 'Lend Me Your Light,' Kersi is almost forced to go abroad by popular sentiment of the Parsi community including his parents. His reflection is self-revealing: "I, Tiresias, blind and throbbing between two lives, the one in Bombay and the one to come in Toronto" (*TFFB* 180). Mistry has been careful enough to juxtapose him with his brother Percy who is an idealist and risks his life to work in the rural areas of India. There are others like Kersi, who aspire but fail to make the sacrifices needed to have his elder brother's passion. He merely prays, "Lend me your light," but the likes of Percy have shunned the ambivalence and acquired an identity, not necessarily a Parsi one but surely an authentic human identity.

Works Cited

Bharucha, Nilufer, *Rohinton Mistry: Ethnic Enclosures and Transcultural Spaces*. New Delhi: Rawat Publications, 2003.

Dhawan, R.K., Novy Kapadia, et al, ed., *Parsi Fiction*. 2 vols. Delhi: Prestige, 2001.

Haldar, Santwana, ed., *Rohinton Mistry's "Such a Long Journey": A Critical Study*. New Delhi: Asia Book Club, 2006.

Mistry, Rohinton. *Tales from Firozsha Baag*. London: Faber and Faber, 1987.

_____. *Such a Long Journey*. London: Faber and Faber, 1991.

_____. *A Fine Balance*. New York: Vintage Books, 1997.

_____. *Family Matters*. London: Faber and Faber, 2002.

Nanavutty, Piloo. 1980. *The Parsis*. New Delhi: National Book Trust.

Uma Parameswaran's Preoccupation with Feminist Concerns in *Mangoes on the Maple Tree*

DEEPA DIDDI
Manav Rachna International University
Faridabad, India

Writers in English of South Asian Diaspora are as varied in their approach and treatment of the subject from which they derive their inspiration. However, they all share a common trait: a tendency to present India to the rest of the world. Uma Parameswaran is no exception, but she does it without either idealising or treating India as an exotic fruit. As we turn the pages of her works, we get lost so much in the characters that we get the impression that there is no writer behind them pulling the strings. They are independent beings having a free existence.

Mangoes on the Maple Tree, Uma Parameswaran's first novel is set in Winnipeg and the action takes place over a period of twenty days in 1997 during the Great Flood. The primary focus of this novel is the life of two immigrant related families, the Bhaves and the Moghes, and the narrative is told from the different perspectives of the family members but Jyoti Bhave emerges as the protagonist of the novel. What is most refreshing about the novel is that it steers clear of stereotypes about Indian immigrant families. The Bhaves and the Moghes are different from the families that inhibit the world of diasporic fiction. There are no daughters being threatened with arranged marriages, no authoritarian parents and no weepy sentimentalism about the land left behind. Instead we have a narrative about a family that has migrated to Canada and whose daily life involves an interaction between different cultural values.

The Bhave family consists of the parents, Sharad and Savitri, and their three children, Jyoti, Jayant and Krish. Jyoti, the daughter is a college student in relationship with Pierre about whom she becomes increasingly conflicted as the narrative develops. Sharad and Savitri try to balance their desire to protect their children as Indian parents normally do, while allowing them their independence.

The Moghes are a somewhat different family. Veejala Moghe is Sharad's sister and she has two children, Vithal and Preeti. Veejala is a total contrast to Savitri. Savitri is able to balance her family and career; Veejala is torn between the demands of the two. The novel traces the parenting and marital issues of both the couples and the differences between the families are presented as differences that exist within the diasporic community in the process of the families carving out a life for themselves in Canada. Parameswaran refuses to be judgemental about any of her characters.

With consummate skill, Parameswaran highlights conflicts and contradictions that are internal and external, personal and political:

> Jyoti shut the door, stood with her back to it, and turned the boy so he had to face her. Then she loosened her grip, but still held his sweater. . . . 'We are getting a bit tired of uncivilized pigs like you. Yeah, let me tell you, our older boys are getting a wee bit impatient with nerds like you, and have formed a clean up brigade. Do you know I have only to make a phone call to get them out to take care of you? . . .' Her voice was cold, knife edged.[1]

Jyoti troubled at this incident of being called a 'Paki' is forced to analyze her relationship with Pierre. She wonders whether Pierre would realise her torment at such racial words: "Jyoti caught herself short as other thoughts spilled over. Pierre, was he the man? . . . Would Pierre ever understand what and how you feel when you have the word 'Paki' flung at you?" (125)

The fiction of Uma Parameswaran marks an important phase in the growth of South Asian Literature as she captures the mind of the characters, the inner thoughts and workings, and brings out the hidden recesses of the human psyche. She is a painter of words, of conflicting choices and of inner experiences.

She explores and analyses the temperaments, motives, dreams, fears and aspirations of Savitri, Jyoti and Veejala. In the very first chapter, we come across Jyoti's resentment and reactions:

> She had not told her parents about herself and Pierre. What should have been open celebration was now a furtive affair. Jayant was leaving first, making her feel guilty for the hurt Dad would suffer, losing them so close upon each other. Dad and Mom wouldn't adapt easily to the empty nest, especially since she was marrying Pierre and not someone of "our own kind," as Dad said even after all this time in the country. They wouldn't be able to take it. Or maybe they would. They were parents. Perhaps acceptance would come as naturally to them as resentment did to her. (9)

Parameswaran delineates the delicate swings of mood, the see-saw movements of joy and despair, the fragments of feelings perceived and suppressed, the life of senses as well as the heart wringing anguish of the narrator, Jyoti.

Jyoti meets her college friend Rick who invites her to the annual concert. Jyoti shows her willingness to go to the concert with her old friends. The moment Rick is out of sight, Jyoti "felt guilty and nervous. And Resentful." (51) She is confused and wonders how she could have committed herself so unthinkingly to anything without checking with Pierre, her boyfriend.

Uma Parameswaran reveals the consciousness of Jyoti through an exposition of her mind in the process of thinking, feeling and reacting to the stimuli of the moment and situation.

> She loved Pierre. . . . And they were getting married. . . . Why then was she flinching at the thought of marriage, why this resentment?

> The finality of it bothered her. . . . The point was that she felt torn and she shouldn't. Love should not be full of tensions. She felt constricted, robbed of her independence. (53)

She is in a fix. Her confused mind ponders over and she tries to rationalise the feelings of love:

> The point was that she felt torn and she shouldn't. Love should not be full of tensions. She felt constricted, robbed of her independence. (53)

The above-mentioned instance and many other similar situations in the novel bring out the seething discontent within Jyoti. This dissatisfaction within and without makes her bounce upon the spring board of life. Many a time, she loses hold on it and keeps oscillating in opinions and choices to decide who she really is.

Jyoti speculates and questions what husband-wife relationship in most cases means. She asks Mrs Khanna, a stranger, "didn't her husband mind her coming away on a long vacation?" (57) She opens up with Mrs. Khanna, confers with her about her strained and perplexing relationship with Pierre. Mrs Khanna finds it very strange on Jyoti's part to expect man and woman in a relationship to have similar likes and tastes. She is surprised and speaks out: "But why should you feel guilty? If you decide you can get along with someone who is exactly like you, don't you think that's rather impractical?" (59)

Veejala, Jyoti's aunt also gives her a sound piece of advice by saying, "Jyo, . . . jump into bed as many times as you wish with as many different people as you wish, with condoms of course, but don't jump into matrimony." (156)

Parameswaran's female characters represent the amalgamation of the Western and Indian modes of female consciousness and assumptions. Again Veejala tells Jyoti:

> We, people like your parents and I, my generation, born and brought up in another age, another culture, know that marriage is for keeps and we are willing to accept a million eccentricities and needs in each other; but you kids who grow up here are so rigid in

> your expectations, so lax in your commitment, you throw in the towel the minute something goes wrong. (156)

Parameswaran highlights the contrasting ideologies of the first and the second generation immigrant women. The first generation immigrants like Savitri and Veejala have 'outwardly' adapted to the alien western culture but 'within' the traditions are firmly rooted. Marriage is for the keeps, as told to Jyoti by Veejala. This requires adjustment from both the parties. Arnold Weinstein says:

> To maintain a relationship over time (formerly known as marriage) entails energies other than passion. The energies in question have to do with fidelity, evolving feelings and the like . . . coming together is possible for anyone; staying together is a challenge to all parties involved . . . for it is an act of volition, the foisting of man-made pattern on the heterogeneous randomness of the species.[2]

Parameswaran highlights the distress of woman in a patriarchal society in which man enjoys every privilege while the woman has to be content only with a few. Pierre cares little for Jyoti's sentiments or feelings. He forgets that Jyoti needs love, sympathy, company and understanding from him. He expects her to be on his beck and call, to be sensitive to his needs and desires. In a man-woman relationship, it is the man who enjoys supreme authority. On Jyoti's asking for time to sort out their relationship and then her subsequent refusal to accompany Pierre to his flat in the afternoon makes Pierre lose his temper. He voices his anger very sharply: "Damn it, . . . How can you be so cool, so rational? He followed her and filled the doorway." (160)

Jyoti realises that Pierre had been taking decisions on their behalf without even consulting her. She also speculates at the lack of communication between them.

> Pierre had made so many decisions for them with such rapidity: Regina instead of Edmonton, a house she had not set eyes on, . . . What had they talked about? Suddenly she realised she drew a

> blank on the last three months except for the sweet nothings of the bed. (75)

It is her protagonists' existential choices, their recognition of the subordination of women and their objective to overcome them that makes Uma Parameswaran a feminist writer.

Savitri in *Mangoes on the Maple Tree* is an exponent of progressive feminism. She desires Jyoti to have all that she could not, but wanted.

> Jyoti, Jyotishma, my darling child, this still core of sadness that veils your eyes, this silence that pales your cheeks, when did you get it, my child, and why? In your eyes I had hoped to see the flash that betimes mine even now; in your voice I hoped to hear the song of the sky that comes even now to me though never so loud nor often. But you, in the floodtide of first love. (24)

Mother-daughter relationship and their ambiguous pains and pleasures have become an integral part of contemporary women's fiction. Adrienne Rich comments, "Daughters instinctively turn to their mothers for mutual confirmation from and with them."[3] In *Mangoes on the Maple Tree*, Uma Parameswaran has deftly carved out the various aspects of a mother-daughter relationship. Motherhood has its own joys and sorrows. The problems involved in motherhood are elaborately delineated by Parameswaran. Savitri is worried about Jyoti's sexual relation with Pierre. She firmly tells her daughter: "I'll take you to Dr. Rogers and put you on the pill." She repeats herself: "But you will go to him, Jyoti," and after a pause, "if you haven't already, of course." (62) Motherhood gives weal and woe, pain and pleasure simultaneously. Jyoti asks her mother if she would feel offended on her 'moving in' with Pierre! Jyoti is shocked at her mother's calm response: "Is that any different from getting married? When you hold a man in your arms, in love and not in lust, you are bound to him whether you are legally married or not." (188)

Through her mouthpiece Savitri, Parameswaran points out that man-woman relationship can become satisfying only when it is liberated from the conventional approaches. Marriage is a healthy partnership between male and female based on respect, understanding, consideration and involvement. Savitri tells her daughter:

> My grandparents, who brought me up, I can now see were so different from each other. But when I was a child, a girl, even a young woman, I naturally and blindly believed they were an open book to one another, that they kept no secrets anywhere between them. (191)

In Savitri Uma Parameswaran has created a highly sensitive, caring, perceptive mother. She adapts herself to the ideas of the new generation, gives her daughter the desired freedom but firmly but playfully advising her with the ways of the world. Towards the end she blesses her daughter:

> Savitri . . . placed both her hands on her daughter's head; then, holding the girl's face between her hands bent down to kiss her on the forehead, combining the ancient rite of blessing with the universal gesture of love. 'All is not lost, my munchkin. May you be as happy as I have been.' (52)

Debra (Jyoti's best friend) sounds Jyoti to be realistic in life. She becomes Uma Parameswaran's mouthpiece to voice strong feminism. Debra firmly tells Jyoti. "It ain't none of his business," (52) Debra said quite categorically to Jyoti's narration of her troubled life with Pierre and its problems. "Quit gender role playing, Jyoti. Does he ever tell you where he is or will be? You say he's in Regina, but did he say what he does on these business trips?" (52) She further iterates: "You've got to stand up for your rights. You've got to develop a positive self image." (52)

Uma Parameswaran's concern of the feminist movement lies in her activist approach. Change is required in the basic social attitudes: toward daughters, toward professions, toward marriage, sex, family and the like. She strongly advocates the need of women to step out of their traditional roles.

> Veejal has always been a rebel, sweetheart. . . . Have I told you about how she sold an heirloom ring to take aviation courses? . . . She wanted to take flying lessons, and of course the family had said no. So she sold the ring and, more than the material worth, it had been given by Peshwa Balaji Rao, . . . Oh, she's done some crazy things. . . . By the time the ring was brought back quietly, for twice its worth, needless to say, she managed to complete the course, quite impervious to the storm around her. (94)

The social inhibitions and the taboos cannot withhold women for long. Her women characters reveal the strife to come over the vulnerability to which the societal and familial judgements subjected them. Veejala is a free thinking woman; her thoughts are with the coming generation of women steeped in a scientific rational way of life. She is a bold, challenging, self-conscious and rebellious woman. Her brother and family wish her to continue with her job as Associate Professor in the Department of Astronomy. She resigns her job, defying authority and security, hierarchy and the irony of woman's masked existence. Veejala asserts her individuality as a woman and also as a partaker in the endless cycle of life. She discovers the meaning of life in her journey to self-assertion.

The position of women is necessarily an element in a total culture; and one cannot ignore the problem that altering an element may affect the traditional whole. Yet there is also an awareness, as Charles Ponnuthurai Sarvan says, "that change is not only inevitable but welcome, that societies and cultures should not be static but dynamic."[4] Cleverly, Uma Parameswaran brings home the truth that intellect is a luxury. Her mouthpiece Savitri acknowledges that one needs time to reflect, to be creative, and to ponder over issues concerning women.

> "I don't know, Jyotishma, I used to think that if I could just take some time from housework and school to think, I could sort out all the questions, iron out all the inconsistencies, and figure out what

> life is all about." She paused and then added, "But I am afraid to take time out, maybe. I am maybe afraid to know the answers. What if there is no pot of gold at the end of the rainbow? Maybe that is why we take up more chores than we can handle, why we make sure we never have enough leisure to think." (96)

Parameswaran gives enough food for thought to her readers. Savitri's dilemma is a universal phenomenon. One is forced to ponder, should women as passive characters put on a hypocritical stance towards themselves as well as the society?

Uma Parameswaran is out and out a feminist. Parameswaran's philosophy that women must find strength in their womanhood, is aptly brought to the fore by Jyoti, in *Mangoes on the Maple Tree*, when she tells Romana: "You don't have to be a boy to be tough, and since you're the oldest, you'd better start being big brother in this house, okay?" (121)

Women certainly must find strength in their womanhood. The need for a supportive male role is evident: fathers, brothers and husbands need to reach out the women folk. Uma Parameswaran's men are blessed with feminine insight and are sensitive to the needs and wants of women.

Jayant in *Mangoes on the Maple Tree* understands that his sister's happiness was at stake because of the rigid stand of his family. He accepts her relationship with Pierre:

> He had loved Pierre once, and not without cause, and therefore could love him again. Jyoti loved Pierre; and if she was not as radiant as she should be, it was because of them—he and Dad and Ma—their instinctive resistance to this alien seducer who had pulled away one of their own. (112)

Vithal becomes the mouthpiece of Parameswaran and through him she talks of the desires of a woman in marriage. Savitri tells Vithal that Donna (the girl Vital is in love with) is sensible, and 'very Hindu in her values'. (92) Vithal responds by saying:

> I don't doubt it. She'd never divorce me, and we'd be a great couple from the outside. . . . But the core, at the core something will be

> missing. A woman, even a Hindu-like woman, perhaps especially a Hindu-like woman, expects her man to be up there, a demigod. They will sympathise with other men's weaknesses but their own man? Oh no, he has to be a kind of Titan, up there. (92)

Uma Parameswaran's women disown a ritualistic and tradition-bound life in order to explore their true selves. Concerned with the women's external quest for an authentic selfhood and an understanding of the existential problems of life, the Parameswaran women are all agog to retain their individuality in the teeth of disintegrating divisive forces that threaten their identity as women.

Parameswaran prefers and seeks altered social and cultural space for her female protagonists with insistence on an empowered sense of female identity. Her female characters search for new ways of life under diverse obstacles and obstructs-articulate conscious and unconscious struggles.

Parameswaran's women represent the amalgamation of the Western and Indian modes of female consciousness and assumptions. Women all over the world share some basic instincts but they have been so moulded by social conventions varying from country to country, that instincts themselves appear to be dissimilar in their exhibition. In fact, the differences that we see between the problems of women in the East and the West are the superimpositions of conventional habits.

NOTES

1. Uma Parameswaran, *Mangoes on the Maple Tree* (Canada: Broken Jaw Press, 1999), p. 121.
2. Arnold Weinstein, *The Fiction of Relationship* (New Jersey: Princeton Univ Press), p. 25.
3. Miti Pandey, *Feminism in Contemporary British and Indian English Fiction* (New Delhi: Sarup, 2003), p. 110.
4. Manmohan K. Bhatnagar, *Feminist English Literature* (New Delhi: Atlantic, 2002), p.125.

Visible Minorities and Canadian Cultural Mosaic

HEDDA BEN-BASSAT

Canadians have often complained that, unlike Americans, they have no common meeting ground or agreement on what constitutes a consolidating Canadian nationhood. Rather, as historian Ramsay Cook half-jokingly said, "we play psychiatrists to the Canadian Portnoy, hoping to discover a national identity."[1] In the attempt to delineate such distinctive identity, Canadians adopted in the late 1960s cultural mosaic as central self-image, which they contrasted with their southern neighbour's structuring metaphor of the melting pot. The idea was first introduced into Canadian discourse of self-fashioning during the upsurge in nationalistic sentiments after the Centennial celebrations of 1967. As an extension of the federal government's policy of biculturalism and bilingualism enacted to appease the French Canadians, the cultural mosaic model aimed at moulding national consciousness through negotiating between a multiplicity of diverse identities—including that of French Canada—and a singular federal, arguably Anglophone, orientation.[2] In 1971, the federal government declared a Multiculturalism Policy, aimed at "unity in diversity." This framework was further reinforced with the introduction in 1977 of the Canadian Human Rights Act,[3] and finally with the 1988 Canadian Multiculturalism Act, which set to weave together political and cultural citizenship. In the absence of a single unifying and assimilative ideology, the discourse of multiculturalism thus became a central component of Canada's self-definition as a nation state.

Yet, as political theorist John Harles has pointed out, the cultural mosaic idea has had in fact only modest support in Canada, causing growing anxieties and an ongoing public debate among both mainstream and minority citizens. The debate has centred on various aspects of the multiculturalism policy, especially on the power politics inherent in it.[4]

My paper sets to examine some of the voices in this debate, centring on those of minority scholars and writers.

Official polls and surveys from the early 1990s have shown that a growing number of Canadians "want the mosaic to melt," and that they seek a more stable and cohesive national identity into which ethnic minorities should try to fit. Comparative surveys show, moreover, that,—their melting pot ideology notwithstanding,—"Americans are more likely to support the retention of ethnic cultures than are Canadians."[5] Over 40% of Canadians seem concerned with the growing numbers of "visible minorities," singling out Arabs, blacks and Asians as undesired elements (and the September 11 trauma has of course contributed to this trend).

Though initially all federal political parties welcomed the multicultural policy, two parties later opposed it—the bloc Quebecois because of the attempt to equate French Canadians with other minorities, and the conservative Reform party, which has called ethnic citizens to fit in, claiming that "preservation of diverse cultural heritages should be left to individuals and families."[6]

Nor has the media been absent from the debate. Cultural critic Smaro Kamboureli—a Canadian of Italian origin—argues that Canadian mass media has reflected and enhanced its mainstream readers' objection to multiculturalism. In presenting diversity as threatening to the nation's stability, mass media has disclosed "an underlying belief that Canada's survival depends upon its being a homogenous community whose coherence is to be achieved through mastery of the Other."[7]

Kamboureli is among the many scholars and writers—both mainstream and minority—who have taken an active part in the debate over Canadian multiculturalism. Those in favour, like Canadian philosopher Charles Taylor, have underscored the significance of diversity within national unity. In his seminal essay on the politics of due recognition in multicultural societies, Taylor insists that recognition of individuals and groups in the public sphere "is not just a courtesy we owe people. It is a vital human need . . . [since identity, is negotiated] through dialogue, partly overt, partly internal, with others." "Non-recognition or misrecognition," he further argues, "can be a form of oppression, imprisoning someone in a false, distorted, and reduced mode of living."[8] Taylor accuses dominant groups in immigrant societies of not being open enough to other cultures, and advocates the widening of horizons so that "the relative worth of different cultures might be evident."[9] He approves of the cultural mosaic model in so far as it guarantees "equal treatment of citizens in a variety of respects . . . protecting against discriminatory treatment on a number of irrelevant grounds, such as race." This agenda, Taylor believes, can offer due recognition both of the equal value of different cultures, and of their respective singular worth.[10]

Responding to Taylor's theory, African American cultural theorist, K. Anthony Appiah warns that due recognition of diverse cultures in multicultural societies such as Canada, can easily deteriorate into a "politics of compulsion," forcing a "too tightly scripted," otherness on individuals who do not necessarily wish to organize their lives around its dimensions.[11]

Appiah's critique, which underscores social relations of power in the nation state, is shared by a number of Canadian minority scholars and writers—ironically, members of the very communities that multiculturalism claims to support.[12] Often highlighting the racist and exclusivist aspect of the policy, they argue that the cultural mosaic model allows the Canadian dominant culture—white Eurocentric and colonial—to gain the compliance of minority communities, while in fact creating differentiated citizenship, ghettoized communities and constrained individuals.

Thus, Canadian social scientist and writer Himani Bannerji argues that non-whites in Canada, are "undesirable others," whose own bodies "are used to construct for them some sort of social zone or prison, since they cannot crawl out of their skins, and this signals what life has to offer them in Canada." Differentiated citizenship, according to Bannerji, creates diversity in inequality which "may support a degree of tolerance, but beyond a certain point, on the far edge of equality, it assets "Canadianness," and warns off "others" from making claims on Canada." To integrate with this Canada," Bannerji insists, "would mean a futile attempt at integrating with humiliation and impossibility. . . . We must bite the hand that feeds us, because what it feeds us is neither enough nor for our good."[13]

Integration is doomed to fail, Bannerji and other critics of the policy argue, partly because of "sanctioned exoticism" at the basis of the mu!ticultural policy. Federal support for the preservation of ethnic folklore, Smaro Kamboureli suggests, promotes the exotic image of Others and their cultural heritages, thereby "locking ethnic subjects between 'here' and 'there' [in a] space where they remain visible as 'others'." They often suffer a crisis of identity, as they "fail to recognize their own image in the Otherness mirrored in the dominant society's gaze."[14] Kamboureli quotes from a poem by Cyril Dabydeen, who protests: "I am not West Indian/ I am not/ let me tell you again and again/ that I am here nowhere else."[15]

A critique of alienating exoticism figures very prominently in the Canadian based work of novelist Bharati Mukherjee. Born in India, Mukherjee came to the United States in 1961, married the American writer of Canadian origin Clark Blaise and moved with him to Canada, where she became a citizen. Bitterly frustrated with Canada's official policy of multiculturalism, which she termed "unabashed racism," she initiated, some 15 years later, her family's return to the United States, where she became a naturalized citizen in 1988. "Canada," Mukherjee charges, "is a country that officially and proudly resists cultural fusion. For all its rhetoric about cultural 'mosaic' Canada is a New World country with Old World concepts of a fixed exclusivist national identity."[16]

In essays and interviews Mukherjee underscores an inherent paradox in the Canadian discourse of multiculturalism, which "renders its victims simultaneously invisible and over-exposed . . . invisible and nakedly obvious."[17] As a writer she felt victimized by that paradox when she was labelled a Bengali, not Canadian writer, thus forced into a cultural ghetto in which she refused to be contained.[18]

In her autobiographical narrative *Days and Nights in Calcutta*, Mukherjee recounts her experience as a Canadian citizen of South Asian origin: "In Canada I feel isolated. . . . I am brown; I cannot disappear in a rush-hour crowd. . . . A brown woman in a white society, different, perhaps even special, but definitely not part of the majority."[19] In the introduction to *Darkness*, her first collection of short stories published after she left for the U.S, Mukherjee launches an attack on racism in Canada, and explains her move to the United States:

> The transformation as writer and as resident of the new world occurred with the act of immigration to the United States. Suddenly I was no longer aggrieved. . . . I had moved from being a "visible minority" against whom the nation had officially incited its less-visible citizens to react, to being just another immigrant. In Canada I was frequently taken for a prostitute or shoplifter . . . the society itself . . . routinely made crippling assumptions about me and about my "kind."[20]

The protagonist of "The World according to Hsu,"—one of the stories in *Darkness*—is Ratna, an Indian-Canadian married to Graeme, an English Canadian professor of psychology. Significantly, the story takes place neither in French nor in English Canada, but on a small island in the Indian Ocean, to which the couple travels on vacation. Graeme hopes that in the balmy exotic atmosphere of the far-off island he can convince his unwilling wife to move from Montreal to Toronto, where he has already accepted a job promotion. Arriving on the island, however, they find instead of exotic atmosphere, "an unreported revolution," (41) which renders the island one more site of conflict instead of an interval of romantic harmony.

Although she wishes to be seen as Canadian and not as a detached expatriate Indian, Ratna is still made to feel alienated in Canada. Yet she distinguishes between English and French-Canadian attitude to ethnic minorities. In Montreal she can feel her visibility somewhat dimmed because she is part of a large group of non-francophone residents of diverse origins: "In Montreal she was merely 'English,' a grim joke on generations of British segregationists." (41) By contrast, in English Canada, presumably the stronghold of liberal multiculturalism, she feels prey to a racism that demeans her and deprives her of any identity:

> In Toronto she was not Canadian, not even Indian. She was something called, after the imported idiom of London, a Paki. And for Pakis, Toronto was hell. . . . A week before their flight, a Bengali woman was beaten and nearly blinded on the street.[21]

Sitting in the hotel dining room during curfew on the island, surrounded by other estranged "non-islanders, refugees" of diverse origins, she curiously feels "for the moment at home. . . . No matter where she lived, she would never feel so at home again" (56).

Moving to the United States, Mukherjee claims, has allowed her to regain a sense of home. There, she has moulded for herself and her characters a mitigated version of the melting pot model, as site of negotiations for mutual transformation: "My literary agenda begins by acknowledging that America has transformed me. It does not end until I show that I (along with the hundreds of thousands of immigrants like me) am minute by minute transforming America."[22]

The sense of exclusion and uprootedness felt in Canada by Mukherjee and her characters, is shared by the speaking persona in Dionne Brand's poem "Chronicles of a Hostile Sun": "I am not a refugee,/ I have my papers,/ I was born in the Caribbean/ practically in the sea,/ . . . I have a Canadian passport/ I have lived here all my adult life,/ I am stateless anyway."

Dionne Brand, a poet, novelist, essayist, social activist and militant feminist, immigrated to Canada from Trinidad in 1970. As a member of the African-Caribbean community in Canada, she has taken an active part in the debate on multiculturalism, accusing the dominant cultural discourse of being "violently invasive and hegemonic, rationalizing all others into subordinated categories . . . trying to assimilate a few voices into the discourse without overturning it fundamentally."[23] The basic premise of Brand's critique is that Canadian national identity is necessarily predicated on 'whiteness,' and that racist ideology creates cultural appropriation.[24] She joins other ethnic writers in arguing that the cultural mosaic ideal exoticizes minorities, dividing them into "little cultural groups who have dances and different foods and Caribana. But it doesn't address real power."[25]

In a collection of poems, aptly called *No Language is Neutral*, she underscores the value of language as a political tool:

> I have come to know something simple. Each sentence realized or dreamed jumps like a pulse with history and takes a side. What I say in any language is told in faultless knowledge of skin, in drunkenness and weeping told as a woman without matches and tinder, not in words and in words learned by heart.[26]

Yet the Standard English of mainstream Canada locks the ethnic poet in a liminal position between 'here' and 'there' preventing her from fashioning herself in language:

> This city [Toronto] . . . cannot tell
> me what to say even if it chokes me. Not a single

> word drops from my lips for twenty years about living
> here. Dumbfounded I walk as if these sidewalks are
> a place I'm visiting.

Brand resists Standard English because it encodes the cultural and political facts of domination and exclusion: "We are forced to live in Canadian English, our own language becomes either degraded or exoticized. Either they tell you 'now talk English' or 'come now, say that thing for me.'"[27] Resolved not to comply with either demand, Brand challenges the dominant language by constructing her own version of English. Her new idiom introduces the cadences and syntax of the language she grew up in—"Trinidadian language,"—into the dominant discourse. She insists that her idiom is not simply an exoticized dialect that further alienates, but a means of negotiating with the dominant culture, making an impact while underscoring past and present oppressions:

> The English language that I want contains the resistances to how that language was made, because that language was made through imperialism. . . . As women and as people of colour we write against that language. The more power we acquire to speak and act, the more we change that language. . . . There is a new talk, a new grammar, a new language being made in this.[28]

Brand challenges the role played by fellow Canadian Trinidadian writer, Neil Bissoondath in the multicultural debate. She argues that he betrays ethnic Canadians by resisting the critique many of them launch against the dominant discourse of cultural appropriation:

> He has appeared quite often contesting the notion that voice can be appropriated. . . .We assume that he is cognizant of colonial history, racism and so on, which makes his disagreement more potent. . . . In producing a Neil Bissoondath, the white cultural establishment produces a dark face to dismiss and discredit all the other dark faces and simultaneously to confirm and re-inscribe that colonial representation so essential to racial domination.[29]

Bissoondath, who immigrated to Canada in 1973, has been a provocative participant in the debate on multiculturalism, and has denounced its policy as one "that has been quietly disastrous for the country and for immigrants themselves."[30] He deplores the damage caused by political manipulations from both inside and outside ethnic communities. In his much disputed, often quoted book *Selling Illusions: The Cult of Multiculturalism in Canada* he responds to Brand's accusations of betrayal by stating that he "trusts no one who claims to speak in the name of the People."[31] He accuses politically motivated writers like her, of turning fiction to propaganda, seeking to impose their own ideological visions on others.[32] His own work, he suggests, is more universal and aims at "telling the stories of the men and women who present themselves to [his] imagination regardless of race, regardless of gender."[33]

Yet, as the title of his book indicates, Bissoondath does join other minority writers, including Brand, in criticizing Canadian multicultural policy in general and the sanctioned exoticising of ethnic minorities in particular. This emphasis on difference, he believes, prevents ethnic immigrants from successfully integrating in the dominant culture: "Immigration is essentially about renewal. It is unjust, to individuals and to the communities from which they emerge, to require it to be about statis. To do so is to legitimate marginalization; it is to turn ethnic communities to museums of exoticism."[34]

Bissoondath, however, finds fault not merely with mainstream discourse but also with those ethnic citizens who are convinced by it to the extent of fully complying with what he calls "folkloric Disneyland." "To play the ethnic, deracinated and costumed," he argues, "is to play the stereotype. It is to abdicate one's full humanity in favour of one of its exotic features. To accept the role of the ethnic is also to accept gentle marginalization. It is to accept that one will never be just part of the landscape but always a little apart."[35] One of the gravest problems of multiculturalism he argues is that it assumes, and then convinces ethnic immigrant communities, that they wish to retain their former identity. He shares, oddly enough, the official view of Canada's conservative party, in stating that the preservation of ethnic cultural heritage should be left to individuals.

Far from opting to live as if he were still in Trinidad, Bissoondath, says he would like to think of himself as "a Canadian, and not a Trinidadian Canadian or a West Indian Canadian." He feels at home in Canada, which "now takes all of [his] loyalty, intellectual and emotional."

Bissoondath deplores the fact that Bharati Mukherjee's immigrant experience ended differently. Like him, he notes, she refused to live as an estranged expatriate in Canada, "clutching the souvenirs of an ever retreating past." Like him, she "looked forward (and not backward) to an idea of immigrant perfection."[36] Yet, while in the 1970s and 80s Mukherjee felt it was impossible for ethnic minorities to arrive at a mitigated position between absorption and division in Canada, and so left for the United States, Bissoondath, believes that now that possibility is within reach.

It can be done not by reiterating the dynamics of power politics inherent in multiculturalism, but by re-considering the existing policy of unity in diversity. Ethnic immigrants should be offered the choice to preserve, individually, in their homes, aspects of their past heritage, while at the same time, "blending them into a new vision of Canadianness. . . . A cohesive, effective society enlivened by cultural variety: reasonable diversity within vigorous unity.[37]

NOTES

1. Seymour Martin Lipset, *Continental Divide: The Values and Institutions of the United States and Canada.* (Routledge, 1990) p. 42.
2. Janet McLellan and Anthony H. Richmond, "Multiculturalism in Crisis: Postmodern Perspective on Canada." *Ethnic and Racial Studies* Vol. 17 No. 4 1994, pp. 662-83, p.671.
3. http: //www.pch.gc.ca/progs/multi/reports/ann2002-2003/01_e.cfm

4. John Harles, Multiculturalism, National Identity, and National Integration: The Canadian Case." *International Journal of Canadian Studies*, Vol. 17, Spring 1998, pp. 217-45, 223, 233.
5. *Ibid.*, p. 234.
6. Anoch Padolsky "Multiculturalism at the Millennium," *Journal of Canadian Studies*, Spring 2003.
7. Smaro Kamboureli *Scandalous Bodies: Diasporic Literature in English Canada*, Oxford UP, 2000, p. 83.
8. Charles Taylor, "The Politic of Recognition" *New Contexts Of Canadian Criticism*, ed. Ajay Heble, Donna Palmasteer Penne, Tim Struthers, Broadview Press, 1996, pp. 98-131, 103.
9. Taylor, p. 126.
10. Taylor, p. 120.
11. K. Anthony Appiah, "Identity, Authenticity, Survival." *Multiculturalism: Examining the Politics of Recognition*, ed. Amy Gutmann. Princeton UP, 1994, pp. 149-63, 161, 163.
12. Harles, p. 235.
13. Himani Bannerji, *The Dark Side of the Nation: Essays on Multiculturalism, Nationalism and Gender*, Canadian Scholars' Press, 2000 pp. 96-120.
14. Kamboureli, p.139.
15. Kimboureli, p. 149.
16. Bharati Mukherjee, "American Dreamer," *Mother Jones* (Jan.-Feb. 1997), p. 3.
17. Bharati Mukherjee "An Invisible Woman" *Saturday Night*, Vol. 96, No. 3, March 1981, pp. 36, 40.
18. Bharati Mukherjee, "Two Ways to Belong in America," *NYC Times*, Sept. 22, 1996, p. 2.
19. Clark Blaise & Bharati Mukherjee, *Days and Nights in Calcutta,* Doubleday, 1977, pp. 169, 179.
20. Bharati Mukherjee, *Darkness*, pp. 2-3.
21. Bharati Mukherjee, "The World according to Hsu," *Darkness.* pp. 37-56, pp. 41, 47.
22. Bharati Mukherjee, "American Dreamer," pp. 4-5.
23. Dionne Brand, "Writing it," *The Power to Bend Spoons*, ed. Beverley Daurio. The Mercury Press, 1998, p. 35.
24. Dionne Brand, "Whose Gaze and Who Speaks for Whom," *Bread Out of Stone*, Toronto: Coach House Press, 1994, p. 158.

25. Dionne Brand, *Other Solitudes*, ed. Linda Hutcheon and M. Richmond. Toronto: Oxford UP, 1990, p. 274.
26. Dionne Brand, *No Language Is Neutral,* Toronto: Coach House Press, 1990, p. 34.
27. Dionne Brand, "In the Company of My Work," p. 367.
28. Dionne Brand, "Writing It," p. 37.
29. Dionne Brand, "Whose Gaze and Who Speaks for Whom," p. 6.
30. Neil Bissoondath, "No Place Like Home," *New Internationalist*, Vol 305, September 1998, p. 1.
31. Neil Bissoondath, *Selling Illusions: The Cult of Multiculturalism in Canada,* Penguin, 1994, pp. 183, 185-86.
32. Neil Bissoondath, *Selling Illusions*, p. 171.
33. *Ibid.*, p. 186.
34. *Ibid.*, p.112.
35. Neil Bissoondath, "No Place Like Home," p. 1.
36. Neil Bissoondath, *Selling Illusions*, p. 112.
37. *Ibid.*, p. 225

Reading Transculturalism in *Shakti's Words*: *An Anthology of South Asian Canadian Women's Poetry*

PUTUL SATHE
Department of English
S.N.D.T. College of Arts and Commerce
S.N.D.T. Women's University, Mumbai, India

In the context of Canadian literature, ethnic writing has called for a recognition of the arrival of ethnic authors—playwrights, novelists, poets. This corpus of writing has directly challenged established perceptions. Francesco Loriggio in his essay 'The Question of the Corpus: Ethnicity and Canadian Literature' explains:

> In order to properly assess these writers, to determine whether they fit, disavow or generally impinge on current models, we must first read them. And we must attempt to read them on their own terms, bottom-up fashion, . . . In short we must think not of literariness but of literature, of a corpus of work whose existence is enlarged or restricted by circumstances (i.e. by the joint action of the consumers of texts and those—ultimately editors and teachers—who propose or sanction official definitions.) (Loriggio 1987: 54).

'Literature' as opposed to literariness and the larger material conditions has been highlighted by Loriggio, and the present paper seeks to understand the nature of this 'literature' as has been represented in *Shakti's Words: An Anthology of South Asian Canadian Women's Poetry*. The anthology has been institutionally categorized as Diaspora text under the broader rubric of post-colonial studies, setting into motion the binaries of home and away discourse which is "socially shaped and socially shaping" (Clark and Ivanic 1997: 14) and therefore is not monolithic but is other locations.

Sumanyu Satpathy has discussed the question of 'beyond' in postcolonial studies and the needy, there are other paradigms within which the text can be located. Sneja Gunew's term "serial accommodations" can perhaps help us understand its relationship to capitalism, globalization and thereby change the old binaries and cognitive categories. 'South' one of the location of the text has moved to be categorized as Global South which in turn points to thinking about processes of transnationalism, transculturalism and about political and ideological links that are still valid in South.

Transculturation one of the central issues of this anthology, which has been popularized by Mary Louise Pratt, denotes "appropriation and critical reshaping of 'dominant' or 'metropolitan modes of representation', always acknowledging that the process is grounded in 'conditions of coercion, radical inequality, and intractable conflict' (Thomas 2009: 14). Himani Bannerji's poem 'Doing Time' is an effort to connect gendered citizenship with the 'textual and the material, the rhetorical and the real' (Thomas 15) to understand the "conditions of coercion":

> They are what they are. They are fully uncovered all the bricks, barbed wires, concrete, chrome glass, gasses, bombs, helicopters, dogs and Wall Street Journals are there for us to see. If we who are not white and also women, have not yet seen that here we live in a prison, that we are doing time, then we are fools, playing unenjoyable games with ourselves. I won't go so far, however, as to say that we deserve what we get. (Bannerji 1990: 6)

Uma Parameswaran's 'The Interview' articulates the enmeshing the discourses of indigeneity, of docile gendered bodies in global politics:

> And she answered their unspoken fears
> I am your problem.

> In me the bodies of those you've stepped over in your race to the
> ivory tower;
> In me the voices of those you've silenced in your climb to brutal
> power;
> In me the sweat and tears of those you have drugged into helpless
> trance;
> In your Urizenic plans for perpetual dominance.
>
> (Parameswaran 1990: 82)

These voices result in causing a rift between "what we know ourselves to be and what the social and intellectual environment where we are 'raced' tell us" (D.E. Smith, qtd. Bannerji XVI). This in turn results in creating a political realm for the subject to generate an apparatus for questioning of pre-established categories. The narratives are embodiments of consciously and critically creating forms of knowing:

> Thus, the enterprise is not simple representational in the sense of liberal politics, just to become central from having been marginal, or to seek representation or inclusivity within the existing realm of opportunities currently restricted to white middle-class women. The point is to shift the centre itself from the mainstream to the so called margin. By understanding "representation" to mean re-presentation of our realities, from a foundationally critical/revolutionary perspective, there can emerge the possibility of making our very marginality itself the epicenter for change. (Bannerji 1993: XVII)

The politics of visibility is central to this corpus of writing (diaspora literature) and the poems in the *Shakti's Words* are narrative, of historicity and experiences of that social being, whose knowledge about herself is her point of entry. Hence the poems reflect what Frantz Fanon claims as the experience of the oppressed and colonized social being where there is the "intersection of all the relations of domination and resistance" (Frantz Fanon, qtd. Bannerji). The margin is not a pure space although it is a space that conceptualizes alternatives and embodies an agenda for radical cultural practice. Bell hooks in her essay

'Choosing the Margin as a Space of Radical Openness' elaborates upon the potential of marginality in the context of her location as an Afro-American woman writer, to create counter hegemonic discourse. However this 'site' where it is possible to imagine new worlds is not constructed as a binary structure:

> Understanding marginality as position and place of resistance is crucial for oppressed, exploited, colonized people. If we only view the margin as a sign marking the despair, a deep penetrates in a destructive way the very ground of our being. . . . Truly the mind that resists colonization struggles for freedom one longs for as lost. Truly the mind that resists colonization struggles for freedom of expression. The struggle may not even begin with the colonizer; it may begin with one's segregated, colonized community and family. So I want to note that I am not trying to romantically reinscribe the notion of that space of marginality where the oppressed live apart from their oppressors as "pure," I want to say these margins have been both site of repression and sites of resistance. (hooks 1996: 53)

Appropriation of space is connected with the notion of agency. Lakshmi Gill's 'Immigrant Always' illustrates this voice:

> We carry
> our spices
> each time
> we enter
> new space
> the feel
> of newness
> is ginger
> between teeth

Questions pertaining to 'presence' and 'absence' are central to marginality and politics of presence confronts the writers with their voice as a variation on the theme of 'woman', Himani Banerji's observation is worth considering:

> The presence and representation of non white women moves from the margin to the centre only to be marginalized again . . . , even

> when the non white women express themselves, an effect of alienation sets in with the very act itself. . . . Because it is always on the borderline, . . . It is always contained within an adjectivized boundary such as "black" poetry, "visible minority" prose writings, "women of colour" politics, "black" feminism etc. This situates our "difference" or constructs it, as it were, through the very gestures of "inclusion" and multiculturalism. They become empty reference as far as the main issue of racism and exclusion are concerned. (Bannerji XIV)

This paradoxical situation is central to most of the poems in this collection. Surjeet Kalsey's 'Migratory Bird' maps the journey:

> No one knows
> which invisible cage imprisons us?
> And the flight begins to die slowly
> in our wings.
> Some of us are drawn with
> the chain
> some lag
> in the swamp
> No sun, no earth
> where to look at, what
> to look for?

'Transculturalism' emerges as a site, which constructs a politicized notion of 'difference' and provides a critique of liberal notion of visibility. The text initiates a process of understanding the concept of subject that can be articulated through a revolutionary agency. However, this is possible through reflexive epistemology and an understanding of power, which as Chandra Mohanty has pointed out is historical and socio-cultural. The texts reflect a kind of multiplicity:

> The diasporic subject lives in a borderland existence while negotiating her colonial psychological repository and her postcolonial consciousness, anxiety-ridden as she confronts her past in order to reconstruct it for the present. The autobiographical subject is not single and unified. (Ng 2008: 43)

The keywords which open up a matrix of conflicting and cultural ideologies are 'borderlands' and the lack of a single and unified subject position. The new global South results in the creation of nomadic subjectivities celebrated in the work of feminist philosopher Rose Braidotti:

> This politics of locations is best served by a non-unitary vision of the subject that stresses nomadic complexity and open-endedness . . . far from resulting in moral relativism, non-unitary subject positions engender alternative systems of values and specific forms of accountability (Qtd. Sneja Gunew 2008: 11)

Tilottame Rajani's lines are a celebration of this 'fragmentation':

> This fragmentation is
> The iconography
> Of a time imposed
> On shifting focuses
> A time moving
> In sections, sections
> Held in images
> This image is
> The bartered God
> Whose broken body
> In our element

The fashioning of a gendered diasporic self in the context of multiculturalism in Canada is to explore the ambiguity of one's ethnic identity. Rey Chow claims that "the goal of 'writing diaspora' is . . . to unlearn that submission to one's ethnicity such as 'Chineseness' as the ultimate signified even as one continues to support movements for democracy and human rights in China, Hong Kong and elsewhere" (Ng 2008: 43)

Transculturalism in Indian Canadian diaspora writing embodies complex configurations and involves "the undeniable impact of the category of ethnicity on literary production and reception" (Siemerling 1995: 5). The contours of ethnicity in Canada have been shaped by the context and consequences of the Royal Commission on Bilingualism and Biculturalism resulting in Canadian Multiculturalism Act. Ethnicity results in the construction of cross-cultural identification and the very notion of ethnicity implies an act of "ethnogenesis" and is marked by hybridity and invention moving away from 'monoculturalism' and static 'pure pluralism' (Sollor, qtd. Siemerling 2). However ethnic writing often framed as 'minority writing' describes a struggle for identity rooted in experience of racism and reverberates with immigrants experiences of disempowerment:

> Wherever I went
> to become a part of them
> They stripped off
> the flesh from my fingernails
> Eyes pierced my being
> like poisonous thorns
> Benumbed, my senses
> walked downstairs within me. (Kalsey 1990: 38)

Himani Bannerji in her essay 'On the Dark Side of the Nation' explores the issue of presence, absence, visibility, identity and construction of 'Other':

> The state and the "visible minorities," (the non-white people living in Canada) have a complex relationship with each other. There is a fundamental unease with how our difference is construed by the state, how our otherness in relation to Canada is projected and objectified. We cannot be successfully ingested or assimilated or made to vanish from where we are not wanted. We remain an ambiguous presence, our existence a question mark in the side of the nation, with the potential to disclose much about the political unconscious and consciousness of Canada as an "imagined community (B. Anderson)." (Bannerji 1998: 127)

Ethnic writing in the context of Canadian literature represents the postcolonial struggle of minority ethnic writers in Canada to effect a variety of changes in Canadian social, political and cultural institutions. This project is similar to the one in which Aboriginal writers are engaged. The object of Native writers has been of 'inclusion' through a radical re-thinking of North American history and subverting the racist history of Canada.

Reading transculturation and developing a multicultural aesthetic is in itself a decolonizing strategy since it "insists on beginning from post-colonial margins rather than from imperial centre" (Seiler 1998: 62) resulting in deconstructing stereotypes and mediating across cultural spaces. In this anthology transculturation is gendered. Chandra Talpade Mohanty in her essay 'Under Western Eyes: Feminist Scholarship and Colonial Discourses' has challenged the construction of a stable, ahistorical 'Third World Difference', which in turn has been appropriated by Western feminists to construct a homogenized and systematic understanding of oppression of women from third world. The biological has been substituted for the sociological to create a unity of women. The category 'woman' that emerges in this anthology is not a monolithic one and the readers are confronted with diversity found in South Asian poetry. The anthology embraces multivocality and "foregrounds personal narratives that illustrate an intersectional and multiperspectival version of feminism" (Snyder 2008: 175).

And finally being located within the political economy of global economy, these voices analyze the complex racial and gendered effects of global economic and political restructuring of North American society. Through class and race, poems emerge as site for crafting "transnational feminist anti-capitalist critique" (Mohanty 2003: 113) based on an understanding of feminist politics of difference, which is not "reducible to binary oppositions or oppressor/oppressed relations . . . [but] is possible [through] the idea of multiple, fluid structures of domination that intersect to locate women differently at particular historical conjunctures, while insisting on the dynamic oppositional agency of individuals and collectives and their engagement in 'daily life.'" (Mohanty 55).

Works Cited

Bannerji, Himani. "Returning the Gaze: An Introduction." *Returning the Gaze*. Toronto: Sister Vision Press, 1993.

_____. "On the Dark Side of the Nation." *Literary Pluralities*. Ed Christi Verduyn. Ontario: Broadview press, 1998.

Gunew, Sneja. "Serial Accommodations." *Canadian Literature*. Spring 2008.

Loriggio, Francesco. "The Question of the Corpus." *Future Indicative*. Ed John Moss. Ottawa: University of Ottawa, 1987.

Mohanty, Talpade Chandra. *Feminism without Borders*. New Delhi: Zubaan, 2003.

_____. "Feminist Scholarship, Colonial Discourses." *The Post Colonial Studies Reader*, ed Bill Ashcroft, Gareth Griffiths, Helen Tiffin. New York: Routledge, 1995.

Ng, Noelle Maria. "Mapping the Diasporic Self. *Canadian Literature*. Spring 2008.

Satpathy, Sumanyu. "Introduction." *Southern Postcolonialisms*. Ed. Sumanyu Satpathy. New Delhi: Routledge, 2009.

Seiler, Palmer Tamara. "Multi-Vocality and National Literature. *Literary Pluralities*. Ed Christi Verduyn. Ontario: Broadview Press, 1998.

Siemerling Winfried. "Writing Ethnicity: Introduction." *ECW*, No. 57, Winter 1995.

Snyder, Claire R. "What Is This Third Wave Feminism? A New Directions" *Signs*, Vol. 34, No. 1, Autumn 2008.

Thomas, Sue. "A Balance of Stories: The Making of a Discipline" *Southern Postcolonialisms*, ed Sumanyu Satpathy. New Delhi: Routledge, 2009.

Performing a Japanese Housewife in Ruth L. Ozeki's *My Year of Meats*

HSIAO-HAN SHARON CHEN
Department of English
Shih Hsin University
Taipei, Taiwan

Published in 1998, Ruth L. Ozeki's *My Year of Meats* centers on two women, Jane Takagi-Little and Akiko Ueno, who slowly discover the path to self-realization. Takagi is a strong-minded Japanese-American documentarian working for a Japanese television to produce a documentary show on American wives and their meat recipes, through which she later produces a striking documentary on the DES problem in the United States. Akiko Ueno, on the other hand, is the contrary to Takagi. She is obedient, quiet, and anorectic; she is also the victim of domestic violence. After being married for a few years, Akiko Ueno undergoes a great pressure from her husband's request on bearing children, which indirectly causes her anorexia. Yet at the same time, Akiko is slowly changed by Takagi's shows. She realizes that in order to gain dignity, she has to leave her husband John and his mistreatment. Near the end of the novel, she leaves him without leaving a word and flies to the United States with their baby.

Ozeki's depiction of Akiko Ueno suggests the social influence over one's gendered identity as a wife. Gender, according to Anne Bolin, can be defined as the "psychological, cultural and social domain of being male or female" (24). Taking from this, gender as a social construction is conductive to the multiplicity of gender identity. Gender identity includes both personal and social components, which are related to one's self-consciousness and the social constructed gender characteristics. In the case of Akiko, there are certain norms for her to comply with, on which many studies have emphasized that these norms function as regulation of a woman's behaviour from the patriarchal point of view. Being a Japanese wife involves fulfilling responsibilities distributed by the government and customs; thus, a wife needs to perform the role of a Japanese wife to become a Japanese wife.

By resorting to Judith Butler's theory of gender performativity, the purpose of this paper is to investigate the performative power underlying the state and social construction. Butler's concept suggests that with which, bodies generally perform themselves, especially with regard to gender. In *Bodies That Matter* she says that performativity must be understood as "the reiterative and citational practice by which discourse produces the effects that it names" (1993: 1). For Butler, the everyday performativity of gender involves similar but unconscious acts of repetitive citation which genders the body as either feminine or masculine as if it were an inevitable product of nature. She argues that performances like drag and parody have the potential to disrupt the reproductive hegemony and the gender hierarchy based on it. In Akiko's case, through a series of state policies and social reinforcement, both the state and society highlight the importance of motherhood and have outlined a certain life trajectory for women that greatly involve domesticity. That is to say, Akiko Ueno's identity as a Japanese wife is the result of her performing as a Japanese wife, yet at the same time, while she is reproducing the performative conventions associated with her gender, she is silently subverting the reproductive imperative through her anorexia-originated amenorrhoea, which suggests a possible disruption of the geared compulsoriness.

Performative Identity as a Japanese wife

A. Japanese Women as Homemakers

In the introduction of *Defining Women*, the otherness of women in patriarchal society is stated:

> Women are constantly defined in relation to men. . . . The status of men and women have been constructed around a whole series of dichotomous categories: the 'one' and the 'other', the public and private domains, work and home, rationality and emotionality, culture and nature, mind and body, autonomy and dependence, to name just a few. (3)

Motherhood, for example, is one of the constructed thinking; it is always known to be related to one's "maternal instinct" (Gittins 71). Despite the biological base of giving birth to children, the responsibility of child rearing mostly lays on women. The universal thinking of the mother-child relation is that women are born to have maternal instinct and many of the women have been raised to believe in their innate duty. However, a great part of the thinking is based on the social institution. Many studies have emphasized that motherhood plays a great part in a Japanese woman's life. In Japan, the case of motherhood is defined as a major duty for a woman. Both the government and custom convey their encouragement on marriage and child-bearing through policies and unitive thinking.

In "Marriage, Motherhood, and Career Management in a Japanese Counter Culture," Creighton points out that many Japanese women have been raised to consider "the domestic realm their foremost responsibility, marriage and motherhood their primary goals" (205). In order to catch up with the West, the postwar Japanese government has come to a policy to turn men into "corporate warriors" and women into "professional housewives" and a "re-employable labour force" (Kanai 7). Even now that Japan has surpassed the West in economics in many ways, the government continues to take the corporative policy which aims to classify men and women into two categories; the men are expected to devote nearly all their waking hours to their employers while the wives stay at home and devote themselves to domesticity. This corporate-centred patriarchy is constructed through a series of male/ marriage-favoured policies, which are described by Yoshiko Kanai thus:

> Japanese patriarchy is made up of the following elements: (1) a system of controlling the family through lifetime employment, seniority-based salaries and enterprise unions; (2) tax and pension systems which are based on the household unit; and (3) the Japanese welfare system, which is based on the premise of a division of labour and roles between sexes, based on sexism. (8)

In other words, the government encourages marriage by suggesting that everyone in Japan is a member of the big family, whether men or women should take the responsibility distributed by the government; individualism in this situation is considered to be selfishness. To strengthen this patriarchal system, a woman choosing to be a so-called "Office Lady" shall not be assigned an important position at work; even if a woman chooses to take the important "general-job" track as most of the men do, her promotion is slower and more limited compared to male employees. Besides, the government pension system encourages women to settle down and become domestic mainstays. Gendered pay differentials is another example. As Ashikari explains, the gendered disparities deepen as women employees age. Except a small number of professionals, "middle-class women not only want but still need to be dependent on their husband's income" (Ashikari 18).

The social custom also favors marriage by suggesting that it is "a key stage which the Japanese believe everyone must go through" (Lebra 78). This pressure to marry, according to Takie Sugiyama Lebra, is imposed more heavily on women. If a woman of wedded age fails to marry or decides to remain single, she receives pressure from both the society and the family; some people from the same neighborhood may question or even form a collective stress by gossiping, while the other married peers devastate the single woman. In other words, this idea is deeply rooted in the Japanese society, which is a scheme of men working hard to promote the economic status of the big family of Japan and women being expected to contribute in part of the individuals' domesticity.

In her essay "Marriage and Family: Past and Present," Yoshizumi points out that after marriage, a woman leaves her own family and becomes part of the husband's household. Also, a married couple is expected to act as parents rather than a couple, which means that everything the couple does is *kodomo no tame*, for the sake of children (183-98). In a patriarchal society like Japan, a woman's life cycle functions in certain trajectory. According to Rosenberger, the Japanese government has outlined the following life cycle for a woman: after finishing her education, a woman should have a full-time job for a few years before she gets married. At marriage, she then should have children and be supportive to the family (14). This life cycle limits one's major life events within education, employment, marriage and childrearing. Rosenberger also points out that in order to have a smooth execution of the concept, both the government and the society help to construct this image of a proper Japanese woman. Media, for example, is one of the social forces that help to "maintain a stable social order that upholds the legitimacy of the state and the strength of the industrial economy" (12). In her essay "Fragile Resistance, Signs of Status: Women between State and Media in Japan," she studies several of the age-classified fashion magazines. Her argument is that these magazines function not only as fashion consultation but also as living guidelines. They define and delimit the conduct of Japanese women, and these magazines, in part, help to construct the image of Japanese women. Another example of the media's purposive representation of "ideal" women is mentioned in Andrew A. Painter's "The Telerepresentation of Gender in Japan." In this essay, he points out that before a program is broadcasted, the program planning team tends to produce shows that speak "in the voice of (patriarchal) common sense, urging women to persevere, to endure, and to sacrifice" (Painter 58). From his observation, he finds these shows convey cultural representations of family and family relations, such as filial piety and obligation, are combined into ideological formations that "legitimate" and "naturalize the inferior and subservient status of women in Japan" (Painter 57). Accordingly, contemporary Japanese women's status results from a consolidated, complicated and purposely-presented representation that cannot be easily removed from discussion.

In this view, the image of a Japanese wife is fixed; being a Japanese wife basically involves one's unconsciously taking iterative citational acts on wifely characteristics. To be a Japanese wife and avert from external pressure (such as the stress one receives from the society and family if the person fails to fulfill the social obligation), one must comply with the social norms and fulfill the responsibilities that the society expects her to take. Through the subject's constant citation, the geared role becomes an innate compulsion that either fits in with the expectation or encourages one working hard to achieve it. Hence, to discuss the multiplicity of the identity of women, it is necessary to have further discussion on the designated roles for women.

B. Theorizing Performativity

In *The Presentation of Self in Everyday Life*, Goffman analyzes people's daily life and suggests that the self of an individual is a social product that involves performances shaped by the environment and audiences. Performance, according to Goffman, is an individual's activity that continually being presented before one or many observers (22). He points out that different social groupings require different attributes to conduct one's behaviour. To be in a certain grouping, one must not only possess the required attributes, but also sustain the standards of conduct that one's social grouping attaches thereto (75). Considered further, the gender paradigm is similar to the scheme. In a patriarchal society, along with the so-called biological inherency, the dualistic definition on men and women can be seen everywhere. Women are often defined as dependent and limited within domestic realm while men are seen as independent and rational; this stereotypical notion of gender is the standard that one being asked to sustain in order to be in part of the gender grouping and not being punished by the hegemonic power. Butler, however, points out that there is no subject behind the performative act. She argues that performances presume a subject, focusing on the performance itself while, on the other hand, allowing the rejection of the notion of a subject. She points out that the distinction is produced through repetition and people's performance of their designated sex and gender. For her, along with sex, gender is not a natural characteristic but a category constructed through performativity; gender is something one learns, practises and represents through continuous performances of the conventional norms. In other words, sex and gender are both constructs rather than something one is born with or chooses to be.

Butler's concept of performativity relies on rejecting the assumption that gender possesses inherent natural meaning. The demarcation between sex and gender is diminished because "there is no sex that is not always already gender"; that is to say, "all bodies are gendered from the beginning of their social existence" and "gender is not something one is, but something one does" (Salih 91). According to Butler, doing gender describes an ongoing process that involves the "stylized repetition of acts" through time (1999: 179). The act of gender is "both intentional and performative, where performative suggests a dramatic and contingent construction of meaning" (1999: 177). In other words, performativity has enabled a powerful appreciation of the ways that identities are constructed iteratively through complex citational processes. For Butler, the illusory norms are disruptive; through performativity, the reality of gender is put into crisis and the tenuousness of the "reality" is revealed. As she puts it:

> If gender attributes, however, are not expressive but performative, then these attributes effectively constitute the identity they are said to express or reveal. The distinction between expression and performativeness is crucial. If gender attributes and acts, the various ways in which a body shows or produces its cultural signification, are performative, then there is no pre-existing identity by which an

> act or attribute might be measured; there would be no true or false, real or distorted acts of gender, and the postulation of a true gender identity would be revealed as a regulatory fiction. That gender reality is created through sustained social performances means that the very notions of an essential sex and a true or abiding masculinity or femininity are also constituted as part of the strategy that conceals gender's performative character and the performative possibilities for proliferating gender configurations outside the restricting frames of masculinist domination and compulsory heterosexuality. (*Gender Trouble* 180)

Deriving from this, the fixed notion of being a Japanese wife involves a great amount of citational acts of the stylized image of the Japanese wife, through which the effect of cultural and state power is shown. Following Butler's schema, one can see Akiko Ueno's anorexia-originated amenorrhoea is an outcome that challenges the implicitly geared conventions that make much of the importance of motherhood in Japanese society.

C. Performing a Wife under the State and Cultural Norm

Throughout *My Year of Meats*, the heroine Akiko Ueno remains a mute and obedient wife; or more precisely, a woman who speaks only in her little pillow book. Is her silence part of performativity? From my reading of many studies, there is mutual agreement on the responsibilities of a Japanese wife to be sweet-natured, take care of domestic chores and bear children. Many studies have proven that the fixity of such thinking is based on the continual social construction. Starting from the construction of state, Akiko's marriage to John Ueno is an evidence of the interference of the state's power. One day at work, her boss walked to her desk and started the conversation:

> "Tanaka . . . Akiko, isn't it?"
> "*Hai*," Akiko whispered.
> "Mmm. What are you working on?" He said.
> She mumbled the name of the strip.
> "Good, good. How old are you, anyway?"
> "Twenty-nine."

> "About time to marry, don't you think? Any prospects?"
> Akiko's face turned crimson. "No," she gasped.
> "Good. Good. I have someone in mind for you. A good, solid salaryman, works for my friend's company. We'll have tea with them tomorrow. We'll leave here at three." (95)

In 1992, the average wedded age for women was 26 (Kumagai 21). In Japan, according to Sakai Junko, single women over average wedded age and who failed to have children hereafter are called an insulting term "*make inu*," which literally means underdogs (My translation: 19). According to Rosenberger, the Japanese government has outlined a woman's life cycle within education, employment, marriage and child-rearing (14). Along with the state policy, there are some social forces that help to shape the norm, such as the magazines Rosenberger examines in her essay and the social pressure received by the Japanese single women. Deriving from this, the substance of the demanding boss's interference is the exhibition of the state authority. Another exhibition of authority happened the day after Akiko and John's first meeting; the boss came to Akiko and said to her: "Now listen. It's fine for a girl to be shy, it's attractive, even, but a man likes a wife he can talk to. Eventually you are going to have to learn to be more outgoing, understand?" (97). The significance of the boss's discourse here is to delimit a woman's conduct; telling her how one should act in order to achieve the image of a woman basing on heterosexuality and win a marriage to fulfill a woman's responsibility that is distributed by the society. Similar representation of the state authority can be seen in the part of Akiko's meeting with a gynecologist who's famous for the remedy of infertility. When the doctor finds out that Akiko's amenorrhoea is a result of personal cause, he scolds her and threatens to call John (80-81).

Despite her infertility, Akiko's performance as a wife is "flawless": she cooks, she stays at home cleaning the house to keep herself busy (316), she buys condoms as John ordered (45), sometimes she even plays wifely cuteness to please John (46);

however, her inability to give birth to a child is a major failure. As mentioned above, child-rearing is among the major events in one's life. A "proper Japanese wife" should be like John's mother, who has given birth and is proud of her husband and child. Due to the pressure she receives, Akiko transforms the stress into anorexia. One example of the pressure Akiko receives from the society is shown in her conversation with the laundry lady Mrs. Hashimoto:

> "Perhaps that's why . . . perhaps he is spending all his stamina elsewhere. Perhaps you have some nice stepchildren in American—"
>
> Akiko lunged over the counter.
>
> "*And none of our own children here!*" the old lady crowed as she relinquished the paper to Akiko, who crushed it and shoved it into her pocket. (215)

Mrs. Hashimoto's interrogation here can be seen as the general public's interrogation. As noted above, child-rearing is one of the constructed norms that the patriarchal society expects a wife to comply with; in order to take part in the social grouping, one must cite stylized repetition of acts. Akiko's infertility gives an access for the social force to step in. But on the other hand, how does the constructed compulsoriness influence one? In her 1993 work *The Japanese Woman: Traditional Image and Changing Reality*, Sumiko Iwao points out that in general, Japanese women are dependent on men, despite their awareness of the unequal social status between men and women. She states," In facing specific day-to-day situations, Japanese women tend to be extremely pragmatic; they are not necessarily concerned with achieving quality with men in terms of disposal of time and energy or even in terms of income or status rewards for performances" (15). In Akiko's case, the female dependence on men is distinct in the book. Upon her departure for the United States, "she withdrew exactly two-thirds of the money in the joint account she had with her husband" (319). Akiko's financial dependence on John not only reveals general women's dependence on men, but also suggests the compulsory reinforcement that subjugates women to perform the socially designated roles.

In *Gender Trouble*, Butler argues that gender is a performance that is unstable and only made powerful by its constant repetition. She asks: "What kind of subversive repetition might call into question the regulatory practice of identity itself?" (1999: 42). She points out that through ways like parody or rejection, gender norms are disrupted. She states: " The loss of gender norms would have the effect of proliferating gender configurations, destabilizing substantive identity and depriving the naturalizing narratives of compulsory heterosexuality of their central protagonists: 'man' and 'woman'" (1999: 187). In the novel, Akiko's anorexia-originated amenorrhoea suggests a subversion of the reproductive imperative. While she is complying with the conventional norms of a Japanese wife, she is silently subverting them. As mentioned above, the importance of childbearing is one of the shared expectations in Japanese society, which indirectly leads to Akiko's unconscious anorectic symptoms. Every time she faced pressure from the state or society (such as the gynecologist condemning interrogation), she "felt the meat start to rise inside her" and the urge to vomit (81). Her anorexia-originated amenorrhoea disavows the social designated duty to be a mother and the idea of fulfilling a wife's obligation. This silent subversion not only challenges the traditional concept of the identity of being a Japanese wife, but also dissolves the designated social role that is based on the illusory gender paradigm.

D. Anorexia as a subversive act

In the opening of the book, Jane Takagi-Little writes a note for the new program:

> Meat is the Message. . . . It's the meat (not the Mrs.) who's the star of our show! Of course, the "Wife of the Week" is important too. She must be attractive, appetizing, and all-American. She is the Meat Made Manifest: ample, robust, yet never tough or hard to di-

> gest. Through her, Japanese housewives will feel the hearty sense of warmth, of comfort, of hearth and home—the traditional family values symbolized by red meat in rural America. (8)

It is interesting that this passage describes a stylized role of a wife. At the beginning of the show, Takagi-Little purposely presented some seemingly perfect families to her audiences in Japan (the Flowers and the Thayers, for example), but once she took up the meat problem in the states, she started presenting images that subvert the traditional concepts of family (i.e. the lesbian couple Dyann and Lara, and the polyracial Beaudroux family), through which Akiko's transformation is indirectly influenced. The multiplicity of family constitution presented in the novel suggests a fluidity of forming a family; besides the biological connection, members of the family may differ in situations.

Another challenge Ozeki raised in the novel is the meat problem whish has its similarity with the general construction on the female image. Parallel to the "growth-enhanced" meat, an external force has constructed roles for women that are based on biological fertility; basing on such constructed roles, women are designated to produce children and the so-called "natural condition" is seen as an inevitable inherency given by nature. The novel suggests that similar to the general public's ignorance of the secret meat poisoning, the compulsion based on female fertility the masses are not aware of.

Drawing from Butler's notion of performativity, the depiction of the multiplicity of family and Akiko's anorexia suggest a destabilizing force of the constructivist accounts of identity, which result in a negative model of action as the displacement of constraining social norms. Butler suggests that the gender paradigm based on the binary heterosexuality is disruptive, through subversive acts like drag that take part from citing the fixed gender norms, the frailty of the paradigm is revealed. In the case of Akiko Ueno, while she is complying with the social and state-designated role as a Japanese wife, her anorexia-originated amenorrhoea challenges the general expectation that lies on women as roles of wife and mother. Akiko's unconscious refusal to eat drugged beef implies her subconscious rejection to the social construction. But, contrary to Butler's models, Akiko's anorexia is not a repetitive act out of consciousness; it is not until later that she was forced to eat meat under John's surveillance and retrieved menstruation that the readers become aware of her rejection of pregnancy. Thus, it is understood that cultural identity, including gendered identity within a culture, is tied to a shifting set of ideals and performs in accordance to those ideals.

Conclusion

Contrary to Akiko's identity as a Japanese wife, the images of the various American wives in Takagi's shows suggest a possible fluidity of the identity of wives. Regarding the concept of bodies performing themselves in accordance with physiological gender distinction, the act of performativity is a reiterative and citational practice that involves contrivances geared and reinforced by an established concept; hence, the story of Akiko Ueno suggests the moulding characteristics of identity in Japanese society. Yet, as Butler suggests, through performances like drag or parody, one is provided the potential to disrupt the gendered obligations. Resorting to the theory of performativity, one understands that the everyday performativity of a Japanese wife involves similar but unconscious acts of repetitive citation which is constructed by the state and cultural power, such as the pressure Sakai Junko brings up in her book and the media influences Rosenberger examines in her essay (Sakai Junko 19; Rosenberger 12). Considered further, this gendered concept not only exists in Japanese society but in all cultures. As Ozeki depicts, this construction based on gender differential, despite all physiological factors, is unnatural like the drugged beef. However, Akiko's silent subversion through amenorrhoea suggests a possible solution to disrupt the reproductive hegemony that is based on the gender hierarchy, which provides an aspect for us to question the rationality of restriction in accordance with the constructed gender norms.

Bibliography

Primary Source

Ozeki, R.L. *My Year of Meats*. NY: Penguin Books, 1999.

Secondary Sources

Ashikari, Mikkio. "Urban Middle-Class Japanese Women and Their White Faces: Gender, Ideology, and Representation." *Ethos*, 31.1 (2008): 3-37.

Bolin, Anne. "Traversing Gender: Cultural Context and Gender Practices." *Gender Reversals and Gender Cultures: Anthropological and Historical Perspectives*. Ed. Sabrina P. Ramet. NY: Routledge, 1996.

Butler, Judith. *Bodies That Matter*. NY: Routledge, 1993.

_____. *Gender Trouble: Feminism and the Subversion of Identity*. NY: Routledge, 1999.

Creighton, Millie R. "Marriage, Motherhood, and Career Management in a Japanese 'Counter Culture.'" *Re-Imaging Japanese Women*. Ed. Anne E. Imamura. CA: University of California Press, 1996.

Gittins, Diana. "What is the family? Is it universal?" *Defining Women*, ed. Linda McDowell and Rosemary Pringle. MA: Blackwell, 1996.

Goffman, Erving. *The Presentation of Self in Everyday Life*. Anchor, 1959.

Iwao, Sumiko. *The Japanese Woman: Traditional Image and Changing Reality*. Cambridge: Harvard University Press, 1993.

Kanai, Yoshiko. "Issues for Japanese Feminism." *Voices from the Japanese Women's Movement*, ed. AMPO Japan. NY: East Gate, 1996.

Kumagai, Fumie. *Unmasking Japan Today: the Impact of Traditional*. CT: Greenwood, 1996.

Lebra, Takie Sugiyama. *Japanese Women*. Honolulu: University of Hawaii Press, 1985.

McDowell, Linda and Rosemary Pringle, ed. *Defining Women*. MA: Blackwell, 1996.

Painter, Andrew A. "The Telerepresentation of Gender in Japan," *Re-Imaging Japanese Women*, ed. Anne E. Imamura. CA: University of California Press, 1996.

Rosenberger, Nancy R. "Fragile Resistance, Signs of Status: Women between State and Media in Japan." *Re-Imaging Japanese Women.*

Sakai, Junko. *Make Inu no Tooboe (The Howlings of the Underdog).* Taipei: Cite, 2006.

Salih, Sara and Judith Butler, ed. *The Judith Butler Reader*. MA: Blackwell, 2003.

Yoshizumi, Kyoko. "Marriage and Family: Past and Present." *Japanese Women: New Feminist Perspectives on the Past, Present, and Future*, ed. Kumiko Fujimura-Fanselow and Atsuko Kameda. NY: Feminist Press, 1995.

Canadian Poets of the Asia-Pacific Region

Uma Parameswaran

Rana Bose

Cyril Dabydeen

Poems by Uma Parameswaran

Uma Parameswaran was born and educated in India. She immigrated to Canada in 1966 and has lived in Winnipeg ever since. She recently retired as Professor of English from the University of Winnipeg. She is the author of books on Indian-diasporic literature, and author of several volumes of fiction, including What was Always Hers, *that won the Jubilee award of 2000 for the best collection of stories.*

Forty Years in Canada
1970

Under a sky more vast than any I've seen,
On snow more cold than ever I dreamed,
I stand alone
Amid masks that speak an alien tongue.
Far far are those I loved and love
And far the fragrance of my native flowers
O'er which bees murmur homeland tunes.
Small comfort I find in these needle pines
That stand bleak against the white.
Where's the fire that can sustain us
In this alien land of endless skies?
Where the friend who'll lend a hand
So we stand tall in our own eyes?
Some day we shall surely sing:
Under a sky bluer than any I've seen,
On snow whiter than ever I dreamed,
I stand beside the Golden Boy
Holding golden sheafs of corn

Against a dawn heralding the joy
Of years to come.

1980
Excerpt from *We are New Canadians*

We are new Canadians
Come from faraway places,
The Alps and the Andes
Essequibo and the Ganges,
Our memories, our faces
Chiselled by ancient cultures
Whose course had been half run
Long ere Cartier's had begun.
We are New Canadians.
Same as the old, we grew
Ten moons in our mother's womb,
Learnt to love, play and pray
On parents' knees.
Tasted youth's sadsweet greenness
And love's silver dreams.
Canada's fields are sown with gold,
Some said, and so it is.
It will not be easy, some said,
And it has not, as we well know
Who have worked hard, or worse still
Have no work at all, though willing
And waiting for the break
That would set us on our own.
What we were not told, never guessed,
Is written on our children's faces
Furrowed with tears because of our race
Or colour, or tongue that stumbles
Over words so alien to the many places
From which we've come.

Will doors shut on them as on us?
Landlords', employers', neighbours'?
Have we come from the Niger and Luzon,
From the Antilles and Hongkong
To these vast empty spaces
Only to see our young ones' faces
Slapped by unthinking scorn,
Unfeeling barbs
From closed fists and closed hearts?

2000
From *Kanishka Poems* (II)
(*written for the 15th anniversary of the crash of Air India flight 182 on June 23, 1985*)

Long a celebrant
of this lovely land of endless skies,
whose earth I've walked into horizons,
whose skies I've flown from sea to sea,
in whose rivers I've seen my own—
the singing waters of my native Narmada,
Kaveri whose rapids feed ancestral fields—
I come, bearing votive incense and a pledge.
I, who have brought Ganga to our land, our Assiniboine,
and built my temples where it flows into the Red,
and where the fluteplayer dances on the waters of La Salle,
now stand on the ocean's shore
and know
I must walk farther,
fly higher, dive deeper
to find the fire
that is now but ember
in empty pyres
that smoulder ever
waiting for the hopes,

the bodies, that lie strewn
on ocean floor.
Earth, air, fire, water,
Progenitors of all life,
Inspire, exhort, goad, needle,
nag us night and day
I pray
That all who live
in this lonely land of endless skies
Remember now and forever
the dates etched in caves of memory
where there and here come together
to make us who we be.
Dive deeper.
July 23rd, 1914, dark day of ignominy,
when Komagatamaru was driven back into the open sea,
while people and papers screamed:
Keep Canada White, true north strong and free.
(as though the first nations of this land
never were, had never been.)
Fly higher.
June 23rd, 1985, dark day of ignominy
when Mulroney sent condolences to Rajiv Gandhi
for "your great loss"
after Flight 182 hurtled through the sky into the Irish sea,
stopping three hundred Canadian hearts
and breaking three thousand more.
Cry rivers.
June 23rd, 2000, dark day of ignominy,
when the criminals who sent limbs and hearts
hurtling through the sky into the Irish sea,
have still not been brought to book
because of a government that drags its feet.
She said, Dark, dark your memories.
Surely there are sunnier ones that shine

thru the spruce green of your prairie yards:
November 2nd, 1949, when Jawaharlal in person
Stood on the Pacific shore and thanked
the Ghadars for their part in freedom's cause.
February 21st, 2000, when Ujjal took oath of office
to the sound of India's drums and dance.
Yes, yes, and I have sung psalms to those.
But I come today to light camphor markers,
stupa, gnomon, pyramid, obelisk,
and to sing dirges to the dead, who,
denied funeral pyres,
shall glow forever
in history books and hearts
of all who live from sea to sea.

2005
This Land whereon I Stand

I am come to a place past a fading collage
of nostalgia for another land where mangoes yellow and red
peeped with wonder at the purposeful spruce spare and tall
against blinding snow;
of protests proclaiming alienation, marginalization,
discrimination, racialization
of women, races, classes, ages, shapes and colours
in language deemed meet
for poetry
and for the corporate ladder we call academe;
of thankless service to various causes
social, political, altruistic, educational;
of secret trysts with the muses moving to music
beyond measurable decibels,
dancing with their shadows as they teased me
with poems and stories to magical dells
that have ever been and never reached.

I am come to a place where the land I stand on
Calls me
To know it as I had never known before.
I had searched and sieved through history texts
for resonating names to suit my prairie rhymes—
Johann Cabot, Jean Baptiste La Verendrye,
de Champlain, Vilhjalmer Stefansson,
oh how the syllables echoed like an honour roll of drums,
and names that are etched in the honour rolls of war—
Allan Edy, 25; James Johnston, 26; Harry Edwards, 24;
James Smith, 27; Normand Edmond, 21; Frederick Watson, 26;
Mark Brown, 30; all pilots in the Battle of Britain.
And met too that nameless woman who from Orkney Islands
came across the seas in search of the man who had sired
the child within her, first white woman to stand on the patch
I call my own, this prairie gold once bush,
through which in travel and travail she sought for help.
Nameless she remains, woman-mother-pioneer.
I did not know then
when the mangoes red and yellow
peeped with wonder at the purposeful spruce,
that history texts had redefined, obliterated or consigned
to nothingness the unwritten, deeply etched memories
of peoples who had walked this land longer than anyone
can rightly ascertain.
Now I walk the land whereon I stand
to meet the past beyond my past
that has been forever, never known.
Aditi, goddess of the seven dimensions of the cosmos,
celestial light that flows through the universe,
permeates the consciousness of sentient beings,
mother of humankind,
I see you here,
Aataentsic, who, seeking for healing herbs,
tripped and fell through a hole in the sky,

and was caught in the wing-arms of the Great Geese,
who set her up on the back of Turtle,
which became the earth we know,
where she gave birth to humankind.
Aditi, mother of us all,
Did the birds walk *kiiqturtut* around you
as you lay birthing?
And when the babies came,
Did they swaddle your babies in *qulittaq,*
spear fish with their *kakivak* to feed you,
and dance the *qilaujaniq*?
Aditi, mother of us all,
Did you send one of your sons,
a sage with knowledge drawn
from the fount of Vedas
to our Arctic snows?
and did he teach the Harvaqturmiut
about reincarnation? that the souls of the good
return to earth again as human beings
and that the souls of the evil as beasts?
and to give the name of the noble dead
to the next newborn so they will be here again?
Nowhere else do we find this thought,
not even among those nearest them,
the Quernermiut, Haunektormiut, Hailignayokmiut,
Inuits with other sagas than ours.
Aataentsic, mother of us all,
I stand enthralled in the presence of your children,
with their stories and myths so like our own,
with names more liquid gold than any I've known:
Tsimshian, Kwakiutl, Nootka,
Mohawk, Mikmaq, Salish, Haida,
sounds that danced to caribou drums
ere the Kabloona came
and stilted their steps,

and changed their names,
and penned them in the rez.
And fed them booze,
and no, let me not go there,
for we dance to the future,
red, white, black, yellow and brown
we dance together around the totem
Maple, so white and red,
and the purposeful spruce
straight and tall
against blue-tinged snow.
Aditi Aataentsic, mother of us all,
Bless us now.

Poems by Rana Bose

Rana Bose is multilingual writer, playwright, poet, and engineer. Ten of his plays have been published and performed in Canada, the United States, and India. He has written two novels, Recovering Rude *(2000) and* The Fourth Canvas *(2008), and is currently working on his third. He has published over 100 articles, reviews, short stories, and critical essays and his works have been broadcast and reviewed by* CBC, The Montreal Gazette, The Montreal Mirror, The Montreal Hour, The Globe and Mail, *and* The Ottawa Citizen.

Atrocious calibrated avenue

An Ode to writing in vain . . . prose in rhythm. . . June 2005

I dish out poems, pieces and diatribes that inevitably converge on the political, personal and sometimes paradoxical
I want to climb an electric pole, but I never will and so I stick a note on it to leave a trail, my scent, if you will.
I write stuff that diverges, converges, concludes and confuses.
My daughter says my language is atrocious and I must make up my mind between Malcolm and Madness.
There is a drain flowing outside my house, against the slope, she says. Take a hint, the drain or the flow.
My friends nod, hesitate and clap because, they know not when the end is near or here, until I say thank you, with a sheepish grin that is cultivated with care.
My daughter says, also, I am an untrained apprentice who needs direction frequently, but her former teachers in Albuquerque have invited me inadvertently.
So I am pleased, confused and vindicated, thank you kindly.

I am flummoxed, tired, forgiving and pissed off, frequently at the same time
which describes the slant towards slipping in errors which are often a catastrophe
which I nevertheless, retain for the upkeep of my other soul, which requires a certain flamboyance, élan and style that goes along well with this very happening in this august arts café in this fine and carefully abandoned district, which desperately needs a tenor sax player under a lamppost at some point, where the sky meets the cobbled street.

I have lived a stretch of reticent grief, hi-life and low episodes combined with unwanted fulfilling-ness, which is hard to dodge, but easy to despise whether I live in pristine Montreal or my beloved low-life, much maligned city of dread and terror, now renamed Kolkata where my children will never be, until a change is foreseeable in the distant future which will outstep the bounds of the past and cross swords in the future.

I eject poems and pieces that flow like a stream of detritus, vidange down a calibrated avenue lived in by scratchy djs and trip hoppy heroes in hoodies who follow hareng and who claim to know much better and reject the soulful characterizations of a life in constant terror. And so I am nursed by children, not by parents, comrades and lovers.
I am in and out of my skin with ease, because the outside is temporary, the inside is more so, but intimidating.
I step aside too often, obligingly to avoid the stern stares of the hooded crew, floating through, making passes, finding clues, passing judgement with venom on my sense of past cool.
I see friends and foe, at the front and rear, where they are meant to be, and my words flow atrociously down the calibrated avenue.

White Moca, No Whip
2006-09-13

I see a man in camopants
Latte in hand
Slide by with cool shades
I say nothing

I see a woman, red shirt,
cell-phone dangling,
go to the washroom, crying
I feel nothing

I see two men, one girl,
Fighting a fly, intensely
La Presse in hand,
I see crisis brewing

I see someone, I knew once,
Cross the street,
While the dont-cross hand flashes
I see the point

I see a granny with a nanny
I see a man in an Audi
5 O'clock trim done carefully
I see blight

I see a young girl
Her shirt says "tickle me."
My phone rings,
My son says,
"where the hell are you, dude?"

I'm done I say,

With decaff moca, no whip
Mos def in the ears.
heading home, I say.

Mumbai Blood

Dec 1, 2008, May 4, 2009

Sometime ago,
When the Brits went home,
They left behind,
some towers,
some houses domed.
They left behind,
Marble cold,
Porridge, cucumber and chutney souls.
They left behind,
Hotels, motels
and bungalows
With a 5-star lore.
They infected the press and TV
With a parrot disease
That made them squawk
the word "iconic!"
At every get go!
Iconic, like the Plaza in New York!
Like the Burj In Dubai
Like the Sears tower
In Chicago.
People who go there are the
People that matter
Or, simply don't care.
So the Taj, the Trident got the coverage,
Got the coverage.
Iconic Taj, Iconic!
Now, the peasants and coolies, so bucolic,

Who built Mumbai,
lay bleeding, bloody
On the platform
And railway lines.
They got some coverage!
No big deal!
Bucolic, not Iconic!
And some silly clods, in ninja duds
Came roping down,
an aging chopper,
And played to the camera,
In raging tones.
Meanwhile,
Them 10 boys with nasty eyes and backpacks loaded
Waded ashore
And did what they did
To mow down,
The gentle folks
Who built Mumbai,
Bloody Mumbai.
Now Obama-nation needs some direction
They need the peace in the Asia nation,
They wanna ban the Taliban,
The same Taliban they played footsy with
When the Soviets roared and rumbled.
Ironic, not iconic!
Mumbai bloody Mumbai
Where Jews, Sikhs, Muslims, Christians
Have lived together with Hindus,
Rich, poor, builder, shopper, sailor tradesman
Before the children of midnight were born
In 1947dawn!
Mumbai, Bloody Mumbai.

Namesake and Volver

June 9, 2007 over the Atlantic

Slowly the skin gets depoliticized
mottled and flaky.
The throat parches over
Beleaguered, crotchety and shaky.
The shoulders cringe
Blue veins, snake rivers
Crawl, where muscles
Once showed off

Slowly, the voices,
of mothers and fathers get closer
To a whisper.
Behind curtains,
Conversations drift
and voices lift.
Slowly, the hope
That inclusion will happen, disappears.
Neglect will not be forever, fades.

Slowly she departs
Skips town,
Smiling brightly
Through the window.
Slowly he says "right"
Raising his head
In an indulgent tone,
The intelligence
Of coffee, spewing, brewing from
a fair trade zone.

Slowly the years amble, stroll and roam
Crissing and crossing

We sit like bored cats
Pawing homeless flies
Waiting
To pounce on
Mice men
Who meander in
From an alley
That sold you
The next gen.
With no warranty.

Slowly, the poubelle cans of contention
Distraction, competition and dereliction
Roll, scatter,
In the alley
Where grown-ups
Once grew
with attrition,
Chewing the fish-bones
Of a millionaire
Who made his money
By imitation
leaving the alley
On a Wens'day morning like that was his innovation.

Slowly valour, surprise
Victory and elation rise.
And then collapse on a beachhead.
Breaking thru'
The first forty years
Of émigré madness,
Many trapeze acts
Many deaths,
Of circus acts with life,
Of crisis before the peace

Of peace without control
Of empire by benevolent madness
Of morons winning
And vermin turning slowly,
In a soil
That is pronouncedly hospitable,
Slowly, the majority vote like idiots
And let idiots rule the majority
Slowly they make films like Namesake
Of Mothers left behind
As Fathers reminisce
And quietly perish
in rented places.
The caress of loved ones
Are submarine gestures
Inert to malignant thoughts and secrets
The bend in the road
Is but a dystopic dream
In a church basement
Where the waters rise
As the dykes give up early.

Slowly they make films
like Volver
About coming back
Over and over
Of returning
With haunting eyes
Grace without tears
About slumped bodies
And dumped souls
Spinning darkly
In a cavernous
Veloute.

And slowly I want to volver
Return.
I want to Return
slowly.

Slowly I want to change the names of the spaces
That I sought to change and volver/return the
owners
to their names.

Elegy for a Chinese (or any other) mineworker

December 10, 2004

(Every few months, perhaps weeks, there is a major coal mine accident in China. Environmental issues are not just climate change issues, but health and safety issues for the poor of China and elsewhere.)

I have an image of a flag
That is soundless,
The wind ceased
Dropped anchor
Left town like in a hustle
Unrehearsed.
I hear sirens, bored but smitten
With a terror of their own
Wailing past a dark breeze
Which was cancelled,
From above, by decree
For a risk, below,
calculated
Inside a canary mine,
Where headlights
Fumbled, clutched,
bent over and choked

till the wet wall itself,
grimaced at the CH_4
and sorrow alone, unable,
could not hold back
the roof,
as lips outside quivered,
till hope flickered,
while the gold on rails,
was lifted, foisted, removed
gingerly, and carried out quietly
and left eclipsed by
the black sun
that fires the boiler,
that powers the turbine,
that runs the generator
that brings in the orange glow
Above,
From the down, below.

Poems by Cyril Dabydeen

Cyril Dabydeen's poetry and fiction have appeared in over 60 periodicals and anthologized in the Oxford, Penguin, and Heinemann Books of Caribbean Verse. A former Poet Laureate of Ottawa, his latest poetry books are Unanimous Night *(Black Moss Press),* Uncharted Heart *(Borealis Press) and* Imaginary Origins: New and Selected Poems *(Peepal Tree Press, UK). His recent novel,* Drums of My Flesh, *had been nominated for the prestigious IMPAC/ Dublin Literary Prize and won the international Guyana Prize for Fiction.*

Nirvana

Swimming in the pool—
my ashram
I now call it—imagining being
in the Ocean of Life

Enlightenment that I seek
most of all, but my friend
smiles as he looks at the beautiful girl
in a two-piece bathing suit
going to the other end

And quickly he goes after her,
calling out to me, "There
she is—Nirvana I'm after!"

Sea Song

In my youth I would sit by the sea and talk of a wedding
—Marvellous it would be

—Underthings would fly like kites
—I would dream of nothing else but love
—The waves would carry us along
—We would be loved ones always

But the sea rolled and the waves came higher
—It became something of danger
—It became a face that mocked
—A thing with eyes like sprites
—It looked back from the crest of the waves

Then I would imagine myself a dolphin
—Ready to cry out sad songs
—Not knowing what else to do
—How really to quell despair
—All I kept dreaming about

Finally I tied the knot and everything melded
—With the sea and ocean
—The wind and the waves became a song
—How it was meant to be since the beginning
—What I always longed for
—Musk of desire really

And we held hands and walked into the sea
—Taking the waves by surprise
—Swallowing the surf and ocean
—Mocking our shadows on hot sand
—Being against the sun itself

Then nothing more was said between us
—Nothing else seemed real
—The waves beating stronger
—The one voice within urging us
—To be where we were meant to be

—From the very beginning

Financial Advisor

The Nesbitt Burns'
investment advisor
talks about stocks falling,
& prices going up;
it's inflation, don't I know
because of places like China
where a dam's recently built
by the Yangtze River—
whole populations moving;
and it's India's turn,
with movement of peoples—
now at our behest, he says.

Such pressing demands—
commodities that keep going up,
& the need for more food
& gas, the world over, see—
carbon emissions, for sure—
oh, those driving SUVs at breakneck
speed; and maybe it's not unlike
writing a poem, Pound's Cantos. . .
to be sure, images forming, but
with the senses always in check.

Now it's the soul's journey
with Nataraja's arms & feet—
in the air, a ring of flames
going round the dancer's body—
Shiva or Krishna—a fortune
to be made with goddess Lakshmi
also at my beck and call.

The financial advisor, more than
        Leacock's bank clerk—
shakes his head, urging that I
        only consider my place
in the universe: oh, where else?
        See, everyone's becoming
emotionally involved or just hoping
        for economic recovery—
if we will only stop speculating. . .
        about a downturn—
the hereafter being all.

Dead White Men

—for Robert Sauve

History's about dead white men,
he tells me in more than jest
        talking about Barack Obama
and America's winning ways—
and his son's now studying
        at the University of Chicago—
in changing times, changing places,
        or laughter always

Another tells of his wife, a junior
school teacher being given a five-day
        suspension because she'd gone home
for a school reunion in her native
        New Zealand—
and she hoped to meet Maoris
        "from way back"—words
said to the Ottawa School Board
        officials who frowned. . .
thinking of punitive measures

        for her skipping classes

I mulled over the *Royal Reader*
text of my junior school days
        in British Guiana,
and Queen Elizabeth's coronation—
        the mug I'd been given—
a memento really an image still
with me in Canada
        like my own treasured gift
of long ago considering—
        the world's winning ways